Kerala and the Knowledge Economy

About the Editors

K. J. Joseph is the Director, Gulati Institute of Finance and Taxation (GIFT), Secretary General of GLOBELICS, and the Founding Editor-in-Chief of *Innovation and Development* published by Taylor and Francis and *Kerala Economy* published by GIFT. Earlier positions that he held include Ministry of Commerce Chair Professor at Centre for Development Studies, Visiting Senior Fellow at RIS, New Delhi, Professor Jawaharlal Nehru University, IT Policy Consultant of UNESCAP for Cambodia, Laos, Myanmar, Vietnam, Thailand and the Yunnan Province of China, Expert in Innovation studies at Tianjin University of Finance and Economics, China, selected under the program of the search for global experts. Gold Medallist of the Calicut University for MA in Economics, he earned M Phil and PhD degrees from Jawaharlal Nehru University (CDS) and undertook post-doctoral research at Yale University as a Ford Foundation Fellow during the mid-1990s. He has published over 90 research papers and a number of policy-oriented reports, along with eight books published by six leading international publishers (Sage Publications, Oxford University Press, Palgrave Macmillan, Concept Publishing, Routledge, and Edward Elgar).

Dr. P.V. Unnikrishnan is a highly accomplished professional with over 37 years of experience in academia, research, government, and consulting. With expertise in EC Engineering and e-Gov, he has played key roles in technology development, the development sector, and government operations. Notable achievements include spearheading critical projects in decentralised planning, administrative reforms, service delivery, and knowledge management. Dr. Unnikrishnan's groundbreaking work in e-governance for local self-government institutions earned him national and international recognition. He leads Kerala's transition to a Knowledge Economy and drives innovation promotion initiatives. His exceptional contributions have garnered numerous awards and positioned him as a leader in driving socio-economic growth and technological advancements in Kerala.

Dr. Kiran Kumar Kakarlapudi is an Assistant Professor at Gulati Institute of Finance and Taxation (GIFT), Thiruvananthapuram. He holds a PhD in Economics from the Centre for Development Studies (CDS) affiliated to Jawaharlal Nehru University (JNU), New Delhi, Thiruvananthapuram. His research broadly focuses on applied development economics, emphasising issues relating to innovation and development at the micro and macro levels and labour market impacts of innovation and technology. He also researches finance and inclusion. He is also an adjunct faculty member of the Digital University of Kerala, Thiruvananthapuram. Previously, he worked at the United Nations Economic and Social Commission for Asia and the Pacific (UN-ESCAP) and the Centre for Development Studies (CDS). His research appeared in various internationally reputed journals and edited volumes.

Kerala
and the Knowledge Economy

Proceeding of an International Workshop on Transforming Kerala into a Knowledge Economy

Editors
K.J. Joseph
P.V. Unnikrishnan
Kiran Kumar Kakarlapudi

Published on Behalf of

GULATI INSTITUTE OF FINANCE AND TAXATION
GLOBELICS
Concept
Since 1974

ISBN: 978-93-5594-781-9

First Published 2025

Published and Printed by

Concept Publishing Company Pvt. Ltd.
A/15-16, Commercial Block, Mohan Garden
New Delhi-110059 (India)
T: +91-11-41101460
E: publishing@conceptpub.com, *W*: www.conceptpub.com

Cataloging in Publication--Courtesy: D.K. Agencies (P) Ltd. <docinfo@dkagencies.com>

Kerala and the knowledge economy : proceeding of an International Workshop on Transforming Kerala into a Knowledge Economy / editors, K.J. Joseph, P.V. Unnikrishnan, Kiran Kumar Kakarlapudi.
pages cm
"Published on behalf of Gulati Institute of Finance and Taxation, Globelics."
Includes bibliographical references and index.
ISBN 9789355947819

1. Knowledge economy--India--Kerala--Congresses. 2. Technological innovations--India--Kerala--Congresses. 3. Kerala (India)--Economic policy--Congresses. 4. Kerala (India)--Economic conditions--Congresses. I. Joseph, K. J., 1961- editor. II. Unnikrishnan, P.V. (Potheri Vasudevan), editor. III. Kakarlapudi, Kiran Kumar, editor. IV. Gulati Institute of Finance and Taxation (Trivandrum, India)organizer. V. Globelics (Organization)organizer.

LCC HC437.K4K47 2025 | DDC 330.95483 23

Foreword

Most of you are familiar with the social sector achievements of Kerala which are very well known in development literature. Despite the relatively backward economic conditions, Kerala has been able to provide much better education, healthcare, and social security for its citizens. These are comparable to developed countries rather than most parts of India and this has been achieved through a process of redistribution and public action. This redistributive strategy of growth has ensured that an ordinary citizen in the state is assured of the basic needs. This very proud heritage we want to take forward. But there are problems.

The economic base has remained relatively stagnant, slow-growing, and less productive. As a result,unemployment of the educated is the biggest developmental challenge faced by Kerala. The present employment schemes are inadequate to resolve the unemployment of the educated. While the national level of unemployment in the age group of 15 to 59 was 5.8 per cent in 2018-19, it was 10.4 per cent in Kerala. The main reason attributed to this is unemployment among women in Kerala. While the male unemployment rate in Kerala is 5.8 per cent, the female unemployment rate is as high as 19.1 per cent. It is shameful to note that while the labour participation rate of men is 73.5 per cent, that of women is only 28.5 per cent.

Therefore, there is always a concern whether this redistributive path could be sustained. Hence, there is an urgent need for are structuring of the economic base and a shift in the development path from low productivity. We must transform to a development path that is more in tune with the resource endowment of the state, both natural and human. Therefore, we have come to the conclusion that the most suitable industrial structure would be the one dominated by knowledge-intensive activities.

It requires huge investment in the infrastructure because, for the last century, Kerala has focused on social sector spending. We are capital expenditure deficit. So, five years back we made a bold initiative to mobilize resources outside the budget through a special purpose vehicle- Kerala Infrastructure Investment Fund Board (KIIFB)—that has led to unprecedented growth in the investment for building physical infrastructure. The total amount would come to roughly half a trillion rupees.

We are attempting to do two major interventions: the first one is to create the global job portal. Within this small state of Kerala,the total number of educated unemployed, including women who are just forced to remain in their houses would come to 5 million. So, they will be skilled through an intensive programme of skilling and placed on this job portal trying to make an intervention in the new drift or shift in the labour market towards say working near home or working at home. Secondly, we would also want to promote knowledge industries within the state. So, we have a very big programme for promoting innovative start-ups and knowledge industries. The basis of all this would be the restructuring of the higher education in Kerala, a very bold programme to change the entire higher education sector.

The government aims to utilize all the possibilities created by work near home and work from home. Opportunities will be created for companies to recruit employees for centralized or decentralized jobs. An extensive scheme is being initiated to provide employment to at least 20 lakh persons through digital platforms within 5 years. Changes happening in the global job market and the fame attained by Kerala in the COVID defence will help in the success of this employment strategy. There was no other time the brand Kerala got discussed even among the common men. Kerala Development Innovation Strategy Council (K-DISC) will be restructured as a registered society with the Chief Minister as its Chairperson. The whole process of transforming Kerala into a knowledge economy will be coordinated and monitored by K-DISC. The knowledge economy in turn will be built on three key pillars-digital infrastructure with K-Fon at its centre, a vibrant higher education system, and finally the Kerala innovation society.

For transformation into such a society, it is essential to have a suitable information and digital ecosystem. The digitalization of schools is a decisive step towards this goal. The new generation can develop expertise in information technology and access the vast universe of knowledge opened by it. Internet will be provided free of cost to below-poverty-line (BPL) families. 30,000 government institutions will be connected by high-speed intranet facility. The internet speed will range from 10 MBPS to 1 GBPS. The government will facilitate the growth of fields such as Artificial Intelligence, Blockchain, and the Internet of Things. E-commerce and digital services will be made available to industrial, commercial, and tourism enterprises including the small-scale sector of Kerala. K-Fon will become a shot in the arm for our e-governance system.

Our next aim is to transform higher education in line with our achievements in school education over the past five years. Several different indicators are now available globally for measuring the standard of higher education. The most prominent among them is the ranking of global universities published by Times Higher Education. Only one university from Kerala figures in the list and the ranking for this is between 600-800 range. Another prominent ranking is by the Shanghai Ranking Consultancy, which ranks 4000 universities across 54 subjects. Not even one university from Kerala finds a place in these 54 subjects. Investment many times higher than the present one is inevitable in higher education. Similarly, the approach to teaching and research needs a paradigm shift. Both are not easy. We ought to move towards this goal with resolve. The enrolment ratio in the higher education sector shall be raised to at least 75 per cent. The all-India average is 26 per cent. At present the enrolment ratio in Kerala is 37 per cent.

To make higher education more vibrant, a number of fully autonomous Inter-University Centres and Schools are being envisaged within universities. The appointments to these institutions will be made from among experts at the national level through a search committee. These centres/schools will develop under the leadership of top experts in the respective fields. Further 500 'Nava Kerala' post-doctoral fellowships are being instituted with support for establishing laboratories and other facilities. These post-doctoral fellowships, with a duration of two years, will be open to experts within and outside the country with a view to facilitating brain circulation.

Innovation means the translation of new or existing knowledge into a new product, new process, a new form of organization ora new marketing method. Incessant innovation needs to be made at all levels for the rapid growth of Kerala. Binder-less board made of coconut pith is a product that can deeply influence the development of Kerala. This idea was born in a laboratory at the. Wageningen University. Foam Mattings Limited had converted this idea into a prototype in their pilot plant. It has been proved that a strong plank can be made from the pith of coconut or from the dust of the dry husk of coconut without using any chemicals. When it is turned into a product on a commercial basis, the change in the plywood industry of Kerala will be phenomenal. This will not only lead to industrial growth but also ensure at least one more rupee for the coconut even if it has dry husk.

This budget puts forth a four-point action plan for creating an environment for integrating innovation in all sectors. Any person who finds a solution to any of the problems in agriculture,industry, service, or business of their locality will have a platform to upload their innovation. K-DISC will classify and evaluate such new ideas and techniques with the help of experts in concerned sectors. In the next stage, Start-up Mission and Kerala Digital Transformation Mission in unison will grade these innovations and ensure mentoring and financial assistance for developing them into products. They will take the initiative to spread these products in society as soon as they get a 5-star rating. Conditions will be created for Government and Semi-Government institutions to buy such products at a specified rate without tendering. There will also be a scheme for providing diffusion subsidies in proportion to the turnover of services and technologies. This is a conscious intervention to ensure that, there will not be any digital divide in integrating new technologies. Start-ups will be encouraged to transform the products coming from innovation promotion schemes into commercial ventures.

Start-ups are relevant not only in the IT sector but where innovative concepts are utilized. Kerala has remained at the top of national rankings for the past two years in the creation of an environment for promoting start-ups.

T.M. Thomas Isaac,
Formerly Minister of Finance, Government of Kerala

Preface

Kerala's unique development experience of achieving remarkably high human development at a relatively low per-capita income has by now been touted as the Kerala model of development. While the claim of being a model is questionable, there is much in Kerala's development experience for others to learn from. This includes but is not limited to, extensive social sector innovations at the instance of social reformers that laid the foundation of Kerala's development and innovations in governance like decentralized development. Above all is the competition between the two leading political coalitions of Kerala to support a progressive agenda and to protect the less privileged through various public actions. The question, however, arises; has Kerala exploited its potential fully? The answer, unfortunately, appears to be not in the affirmative.

In this context, the blueprint for development presented by Former Finance Minister Dr. T.M. Thomas Isaac, in his last budget could help Kerala exploit its potential and become yet another contribution for others to emulate. The blueprint is the manifestation of a realistic understanding of one of the core issues of Kerala's development problem—the growing unemployment of educated manpower, especially women. At the core of the budget is the most innovative strategy of transforming Kerala into an inclusive knowledge economy as a conduit for creating employment opportunities for the educated unemployed including women, by harnessing modern technology. This strategy is also a reflection of the perspective that the government holds towards the fourth industrial revolution and its commitment to making use of the new opportunities offered by it in a manner that excludes none.

The knowledge economy, as envisaged by the finance minister, stands on three key pillars. The first one is the IT Infrastructure—including hardware, software, and communication network. Kerala, being a state that set the model for other states to emulate by establishing a state-level electronic development corporation in the early 1970s (KELTRON) and establishing the first technopark in the country, is visualizing the re-emergence of an electronic system design and manufacturing sector in the country when the electronics production base in India becoming weaker, thanks to "Globalization, not in our terms and not in our pace". With innovations associated with Artificial Intelligence, Machine Learning, Robotics and others those segments of the software industry surviving on the labour arbitrage will have to redefine and reposition themselves and the budget underlines the need for such a transformation.

The second pillar is the human capital. Though the State is known for its commitment towards human capital formation and investment in higher education, there is reason to believe that the public returns to such investment have been limited on account of the migration of skilled manpower out of the state. It is in this context that the budget envisages a revamping of the higher education system in the state and to re-skill and up-skill the labour force for the new economy. The third pillar, perhaps the central one of the knowledge economies, is a vibrant innovation system. The budget recognizes that the "key resource in the modern economy is knowledge and if knowledge is the key resource, learning is the key process" as observed by eminent innovation scholars like Lundvall. It is in this context that various initiatives are being laid down in the budget towards building an innovation system at the regional and sectoral level at the instance of the Kerala Development and Innovation Strategic Council (K-DISC).

There is hardly any economy that is not knowledge-based. However, a knowledge economy is different in the sense that it is based increasingly on knowledge-intensive activities, implying greater reliance on intellectual capital rather than physical inputs. Hence, unlike the traditional economy wherein land, labour, capital and organization are considered basic factors of production, 'knowledge' is the key resource in a knowledge-based economy. The knowledge could be scientific which is often codified and an outcome organised scientific inquiries. In contrast is the synthetic knowledge which is often experience-based and remains tacit and uncodified.

The key challenges in transforming Kerala to a knowledge economy include: First, creating an institutional architecture that facilitates learning of individuals and organisations regardless of their economic and social status.

Secondly, and more importantly, to ensure that all types of knowledge are fully utilized to guarantee an inclusive knowledge economy with shared prosperity. Kerala Budget 2021-22 aimed at addressing these challenges by building the infrastructure for the knowledge economy, and innovation system and facilitating the process of skilling, re-skilling and upskilling.

Addressing these challenges is easier said than done because the road ahead is rocky. Hence, Gulati Institute of Finance and Taxation (GIFT) organised an international consultation towards contributing to the know-how of transforming Kerala into a knowledge economy by harnessing its unique characteristics. Jointly organized with GLOBELICS (an international network of innovation scholars; www.globelics.org), the consultation was inaugurated by the Chief Minster of Kerala, Shri Pinarayi Vijayan with the active involvement of Prof. Thomas Isaac, Finance Minister of Kerala. Reputed scholars, senior policy-makers, and technocrats also contributed to the discourse. The deliberations and sharing of experience by the scholars of eminence from 24 countries from Japan to Costa Rica was especially insightful. This book intends to present succinctly the outcome of the international consultation The issue is broadly organized into three parts. It opens with the addresses that set the context for the new vision for Kerala. The second part articulates the key pillars of the knowledge economy and the reflections from scholars of eminence followed by the last part that highlights the way forward.

While we thank all those who participated for sharing their insights, we are especially thankful to Prof. Vijaya Mohan Pillai, Dr. U.P. Anil Kumar, and the Young Scholars' Forum in GIFT led by Jerome Joseph.

K.J. Joseph
P.V. Unnikrishnan
Kiran Kumar Kakarlapudi

Contents

Part I

Knowledge Economy: Setting the Context

Democratizing Digital Space, the Prelude to Transforming Kerala into a Knowledge Economy

Pinarayi Vijayan

The Government of Kerala has a vision and is committed to turning the same into a reality. Our vision is not a distant dream. But a time-bound plan to realize the aims. We cannot wait long. Here and now we start our leap towards transforming Kerala into a knowledge economy. When we say this, it may appear to many that we are daydreaming or being Utopian. It is neither. We have a plan and we need suggestions and expertise to operationalize it. Our budget which was presented on 15 January 2021, had unveiled plans for transforming Kerala into a knowledge economy. When we say, Kerala has to become a destination for good quality higher education, if there are skeptics, they need to take a brief look at our history. They can see the pioneering efforts taken in making primary education universal. Our initiatives in the field of higher education have also a history of one and a half years. We have initial comparative advantages like high literacy rates and basic technical skills in certain sectors. We need to start on this and build the base for a knowledge economy.

The world is witnessing fast changes. Factories and assembling units, the face of the modern industry have given way to the service sector and innovation-

---

Text of the inaugural address delivered by Shri Pinarayi Vijayan, Chief Minister of Kerala.

induced production process. Internet and connectivity have brought about a sea change in the way we work and how work is being organized. One can stay connected and work in tandem with others from his home or any other place of his choice. Certain countries of the world have transformed themselves into knowledge economies and this knowledge diffused fast to other parts of the world. While saying this, I am not ignoring the inequalities of opportunities often called the digital divide, which impede the entry of many into the world of connectivity.

We fully appreciate the fact that the state has to provide the brick-and-mortar to build the bridge to cover the divide, which has closed the door of the digitalized world to many. The Government of Kerala has recognized access to the internet as a citizen's right and is committed to providing free internet to the poor and at an affordable rate to others through our project called K-FONE. We recognize that democratizing the digital space is the first step to transforming our state into a knowledge economy. We want to encourage research in new and sunrise areas and transform them into innovations that will catalyze our economic growth. We propose to establish centres of excellence in various fields of learning and create an eco-system that will attract the best talents from all over the world. If we could achieve quality schooling, nothing can prevent us from upgrading the quality of our higher education and transforming Kerala into a knowledge economy.

People who graduated from our institutions have become world famous. The list is long and I am not venturing into the exercise of citing names. The aim is to make Kerala a destination for quality higher education. I assure you that you have a government that cares for this. I look forward to your valuable suggestions in making our aim a reality in the shortest possible time. I am not elaborating any further. With utmost happiness, I declare this meeting open.

Thank you.

Knowledge Economy based on Kerala's Unique Strengths

Bengt Ake Lundvall

Only once before, have I been in this unique situation to have a chance to discuss the knowledge economy with a Prime Minister. It was in Lisbon in the year 2000 together with Luc Soete who is on the programme later today. We were invited by the Prime Minister of Portugal to discuss how to develop a long-term strategy for Europe. One of the main themes was to establish knowledge-based development in Europe. The then Prime Minister is not completely unknown to you. It was Antonio Guterres, now the Secretary General of the United Nations.

From the very beginning, there were two competing framings over economic policies. One was a knowledge economy framing which aimed at more and better jobs through investments in knowledge and through building what we call egalitarian learning economies. But the other one was a neo-liberal framing aiming at more jobs, through structural reform and weakening the position of workers in labour markets through what is called 'flexibilization'. Halfway through the planning period, it became clear that the neoliberal view had become the dominant. Within governments, it is normally propagated by the Ministry of Finance (I am happy to note that this is not the case in Kerala!). The neoliberal turn resulted in a much weaker emphasis on building a knowledge economy and it implies that governments looked at labour, not as people or

---

Bengt Ake Lundvall is a Professor Emeritus at Aalborg University Business School, Denmark, and Founder of GLOBELICS. **E-mail:** bal@business.aau.dk

humans who know things and can do things—labour is seen just as a number. And this is the view which prevailed.

In 2003, I was invited to China to become a Professor at Tsinghua University in Beijing. During this period, I realized that the Chinese people had inherited a culture with great respect for knowledge. When this was combined with policies promoting science and innovation, it resulted in a very strong investment in innovation and knowledge. To some degree that has to do with the fact that most of the leaders in China, had education in science or engineering, not like in the West, in economics or law. The main reason why China today can aspire to become the world leader in strategic technologies such as artificial intelligence is massive investment in knowledge and infrastructure and the willingness of ordinary people to invest in education.

One of the things I think is utterly important to the concept of knowledge economy is a broad understanding. I think that in Europe, China, and the United States there is a tendency to understand knowledge as closely related to science and high technology. This means that scientists, engineers, and Research and Development (R&D) managers are seen as the main actors. In the education system, there is a strong focus on universities. I think there are two reasons why one should be aware that this perspective is too narrow and therefore problematic. One is economic and the other one is political. From the economic angle, the diffusion and use of technologies, which is what results in economic development and social well-being,is contingent on the skills and competencies of workers and farmers apart from those of scientists and engineers. Second, from the political angle a knowledge strategy that only promotes academic training risks the alienation of the majority of citizens and creates social and political polarization.

Knowledge is more than science and information. It is important to know about the world of scientists and experts—what we call the wold of "know why "and "know what" knowledge. But it is at least as important as the "know how" to change the world. All of us have elements of know-how. The housewife's skills are important to determine the health and well-being of the family. Workers', fishermen's, and farmers' skills are critical for making use of new technology. Skilled workers', technicians', and designers' skills are crucial for absorbing and adapting to new technology. Managers' and public servants' skills are crucial for the performance of private and public organizations.

So, I want to emphasize that know-how should be regarded as a very important part of knowledge when we talk about the knowledge-based economy. Therefore, and I think very much that this is in line with the thinking of Kerala as I just heard it presented by the Minister of Finance, the knowledge economy is for all and there is a need for lifelong learning. It is important to understand that all people know. The concept of unskilled workers is wrong. There are no unskilled workers. We are all working with different levels and kinds of skills. And everybody has the potential to contribute to the knowledge economy.

One implication is that investment in formal knowledge in the form of education and research should be combined with building 'learning organizations'. We should try to design organizations in private and public sectors in such a way that people learn from what they do and that they get strong incentives to learn from what they do. As I mentioned before, in the neoliberal economic models, labor is reduced to a number, but it is not the number. It is humans with many qualities which can be further developed. Of course, this is general, but I think fits well into the Kerala model.

Concepts such as knowledge economy, learning economy, and national innovation systems draw upon theoretical reflection and empirical research from very different parts of the world. But before applying such concepts and transforming them into political action, I think it is necessary to give full attention to the reality of Kerala. I believe very much in pragmatism, which means that the focus should be on what works best. I think this has to do with how you mix market with plan, the private to the public, and the openness of the economy *versus* protection. It is more helpful to have pragmatism as a basic approach rather than specific narrow and rigid ideological principles.

I have had the pleasure and it was fascinating to read the budget speech for 2021-22, which is a wonderful contrast in style to standard documents from mainstream Ministry of Finance documents. The budget speech is ambitious. There is a strong focus on higher education and research related to science, technology, engineering, and management. But there is also, which I find extremely interesting, a strong gender perspective on the knowledge economy.

I think when you build a knowledge economy in Kerala; you should start from the unique strength of Kerala. You should mobilize social entrepreneurship and grassroots organizations in the transition. You should leave room for local experimentation and I think that you already do that. That is one of your specific ways of governance; you leave room for local and regional experiments and draw lessons from what works in different parts of Kerala. Make visible successful efforts for individuals, organizations, and enterprises, and use them as good examples showing that it pays off to make extraordinary efforts. Mobilize knowledge and build skills with equal opportunities, disregarding gender, ethnicity class, caste, and religion build trust in society, and aim at zero tolerance of corruption and abuse of power. I think these are very much in line with how things are done already in Kerala.

Social sustainability is important to transform towards a knowledge economy with social cohesion. Ecological sustainability is an important change with respect for the natural environment, not just treating natural resources in nature as a kind of input in the production process, but showing some respect for the environment. Economic sustainability is to eradicate poverty and create better jobs and cultural sustainability is to modernize and transform society with respect for cultural heritage.

I am extremely proud in taking part in this communication. I think it is nothing less than a historical moment that the Chief Minister and the Minister of Finance take time off to think creatively about how to use wisdom and knowledge to transform Kerala. It is great and I am very, very happy about this initiative. Thank you very much.

Strengthening the Learning and Research Base

V.K. Ramachandran

If Kerala is on the map today for its outstanding achievements in the overall field of development, a large part of that progress must be attributed to the emphasis that public action paid to the State led formal education. The combination of land reform and formal education, referred to by Professor Isaac, and the freedom and progress that comes from that have been the basis of the progress of our State concerning health, social welfare, and the growth of disposable incomes. Our international participants should also know that Kerala also has the highest per capita consumer expenditure among all the states in India. So that is developed from our progress in what we have called human development indicators. Progress has been most striking in school education, of course, in the 1980s and onwards Kerala is the only state that fulfilled investment levels in school education, that were comparable to that of South Korea, Japan, Taiwan etc. In recent years, the impact of the present government policy and the investments that have been made in upgrading infrastructure and the quality of education, have been extraordinary.

One of the most striking developments in India is public education scenario over the last five years, and perhaps over a much longer period is that since 2017,

---

Prof. V.K. Ramachandran is the Vice-Chairperson of Kerala State Planning Board, Government of Kerala. **E-mail:** gokilapuram@gmail.com more than 5,00,000 school pupils in the state of Kerala have transferred from the fee-paying private system to government schools. Now this is an extraordinary situation to compare what exists in the rest of India. To the sparkling modern structure that now exists in many parts of the state with new desks and school furniture with electronic whiteboards in schools. This is surely one of the most moving and perhaps most important signs of what can be achieved by a combination of investment, political will, and people's participation in the field of knowledge. The Chief Minister mentioned briefly something about experience in higher education, and I see Professor Isaac, but despite our progress, despite our history, the overall experience has been that the state is yet to establish itself as an outstanding location for higher learning and research.

The knowledge economy must be based on a strong, independent flourishing, and inclusive system of higher education with systematic, that is not *ad hoc* state support. It is, as Professor Lundvall said that may not be a sufficient condition, but certainly, this is a necessary condition for our knowledge economy and knowledge society.

The broad themes that are of immediate importance to us in the area of higher education are as follows. One is the whole problem with higher education finance. This is an enormous problem, particularly in the state of an economic structure where we are perpetually in a state of financial stringency and difficulties. Take, for instance, a university that serves in the northern district, Kannur University. We spend about Rs. 75 crore on non-plan and Rs. 22 crore on plan expenditure. This is what we allocate to or what we spend on something else. So the plan expenditure that we allocate to a university that serves about 25,000 to 30,000 people on the main campus and is accountable to about 1,50,000 people altogether. We spend only about Rs. 22 crore on the plan and about Rs. 75 crore on regular expenditure in a year. How we are going to break through this is an enormous question.

The second area is that of curricular innovation strategies to strengthen our specific disciplinary knowledge, while simultaneously introducing methodological development from other disciplines at later stages of education in the higher education system. The third area is trying to explore how new technologies of instruction move for instance, but can best be introduced in colleges and universities and set up inter-university groups for sharing knowledge.

The next area which is very important for us is institutional innovation. Learning from and establishing successful institutional innovations to make Kerala's universities academically autonomous and develop flexible administrative regulations that are transparent and responsive to the requirements of teachers and students. The next area in which we are trying to study and concentrate our attention is networks for teaching, research, and student exchange which is to substantially expand our national and transnational networks for teaching, research, and student exchange. We are looking very seriously at how to expand innovations in libraries, technology, and information availability to college students, and university students all over the state. Finally, we need to retain and strengthen the socially inclusive character of higher education, which is our historical heritage and legacy.

We recognize the crucial role that skill training and development play. We have certain strengths here. A relative abundance of educated and skilled workers, a long history of entrepreneurship, and exposure to the wider world. We are quite interested in some of the International Labour Organization (ILO) proposals in the area of skill development and employability, particularly the need to link training to current labour market needs as well as anticipating and building competencies for jobs for the future. A key aspect of the ILO framework is to expand access to formal employment-related training to equip women and men to work in the formal economy.

Let me end by saying that there is a combination in Kerala particularly of government will from above and the civic cooperation in peoples participation from below. These are joined together, as I believe they will now join in our striving for a knowledge economy for a better system of higher education and a huge improvement in the system of skill development. Then that force in this state becomes unstoppable.

Thank you very much, I wish you all success inthis deliberations, and I look forward to learning from the results of your deliberations.

Knowledge-based Vision for the Future of Kerala

K.M. Abraham

Precisely eight days back, we saw a historic budget being unveiled in the legislative assembly hall. It is painting a vision for the future of Kerala before us. This vision is focused on the theme of knowledge economy, Kerala attaining the kind of heights and position on the international map as the frontier place for knowledge economy.

My thoughts go back to the budget speech wherein I find that the ingredients of the knowledge economy are beautifully captured. Currently, knowledge economy is a very overused word and is underachieved as well. One of the things that has baffled me about the idea of a knowledge economy is that there is no starting point and no ending point. When do we start becoming a knowledge economy and when do we end up becoming a knowledge economy? That is a million-dollar question and I do not think there is a very definite specific answer, at least in the limited readings that I have done. Therefore, I come to the inference that the whole idea of the knowledge economy is a moving target. The target keeps moving and as a society, you have to keep on addressing that transition and dynamically pursue it.

Now in the last few budgets, I would say, you could see that the state has taken some very important steps to finally conclude this Budget 2021-22, that it is time for the state to make this big leap.

Dr. K.M. Abraham is the Chairman of the Kerala Development and Innovation Strategic Council (K-DISC). **E-mail:** chairman@kdisc.kerala.gov.in

Looking at the literature, we can find that Kerala is approaching close to the necessary condition to move towards a knowledge economy. Most of the knowledge economy transitions, we find in states, in regions and in economies, where the service sector is a predominant part of the domestic product. And here we have exactly achieved that. The other one is the society that promotes a learning culture. And I can say in Kerala, probably one of the things that stands out is its questioning mind, its discerning mind, its very insightful mind that the society in Kerala as such can collectively boast of. The third element is about the society that is willing to make significant investments in higher education. The fourth ingredient I would say, is the level of evolution of connectivity in terms of internet connectivity, in terms of telephone connectivity that characterizes the society. I think on all these four ingredients, we are at a stage wherein we will be soon achieving the degree of necessary conditions.

Now, at this juncture, assume a scenario where we would not have focused on the knowledge economy. Kerala at some point in time, like any other society, will become a knowledge society. So what this Budget, actually does is compress the gestation period for this big leap and that is where the tricky part comes in. It is not an easy job. After the budget was announced, a few of us have been meeting and deliberating about what is the next step.

We are particularly happy that our efforts in the last three years are bringing innovation in several spheres. We have now about 1000-1500 students selected for their innovative projects. We have a couple of social projects which are happening in various districts of Kerala. We have some innovation programmes for differently abled children, and we have about 20 very high-tech emerging technology initiatives and innovations, that are going on. Perhaps one of the reasons why the Honourable Finance Minister chose K-DISC as a coordinating agency for bringing in the various aspects of skill, or meeting skill deficiencies and improving the skill base of the state perhaps comes out from this recognition. The K-DISC that we are going to get transformed into is going to be chaired by the Honourable Chief Minister, it will comprise very key ministers of the Council, and it will have the Vice-Chairman of the Planning Board, the Vice-Chancellors of the universities and the directors and the CEOs of the key skill or research institutions of the state.

Now, over the last eight days, I would say me and my colleagues have been trying to find out the appropriate design for a skill portal that will essentially focus not only on conventional skills but on what are the things that we need to address when we plan for the transition of the state into a knowledge economy. One of the mandates that the Honourable Chief Minister has given us in the meeting is that we have got to hit the road running and we got to start and launch this programme in the first or the second week of February. We are gearing towards organizing a very generic skill platform without getting ourselves logged into rigidities or specificities so that the platform can grow organically, interact with the thousands of institutions and local communities in Kerala and probably, be one of the first decentralized skill platforms in the world. That is the aim that we have set for ourselves now. I am confident and sure that the deliberations of this seminar will be of great and invaluable strength.

Thank you very much. I wish the seminar all success.

Thank you.

IT Stimulus for the Knowledge Economy

Deepu Zacharia

I would like to start by saying to Dr Thomas Isaac, that the promises and the very foundation for laying down this knowledge economy as a roadmap for Kerala is welcomed by the IT industry of Kerala, thank you Sir. Before I go into the very ideology of emerging economy, knowledge, tourism and IT, all this will need a stimulus to start the growth and the stimulus is exactly what Kerala as a state is searching for in all of us. The budget is certainly aligned with this stimulus. And for a better understanding of what I am going to focus on in this special address today, I am supposed to be focusing on the IT industry because I come from there.

I want to put down some numbers. The IT spending globally, if I look at traditional and new technologies put together for the year 2019, stood at a staggering 3816 billion US dollars. In 2020, it had a small dip and it went to 3609 billion US dollars. But in 2021 it is supposed to be growing to 3755 billion US dollars. In India, the market size for IT in 2019-20 was about 191 billion US dollars aiming for 350 billion US dollars by 2025. This means that 8 per cent of India's GDP is being contributed by 0.34 per cent of the population (4.4 million IT techies). This is the highest in the world for the concentration of IT talent in one single country.

Deepu Zacharia is joint Secretary, Group of Technology Companies (G-TECH) Kerala.
E-mail: deepu.zacharia@rcggs.com

Where does Kerala stand? Three billion in revenue from IT, 1.5 per cent of the Indian IT population comes from Kerala. Developed markets have high costs and high revenues, but Kerala has high costs and low revenue. How do we counter this? This is the bigger question that we have in front of us on how to derive this knowledge economy.

Let me compare two geographic locations—Kerala and New Zealand. The population of both these locations is spread to 34 million in Kerala and 5 million in New Zealand. The GDP of Kerala is 140 billion dollars, whereas in New Zealand, it is 193 billion dollars. The productivity is 4,170 US dollars *versus* 38,600. What are the sectors that we work in? The sectors that we are working on in Kerala are agriculture, tourism, IT and manpower exports whereas if you look at New Zealand, it is agriculture, tourism, and dairy products alone. So IT is the biggest boost that we have in Kerala that needs to be tapped for boosting the economy.

About 30 per cent of the total population of companies like Infosys, Microsoft, and Wipro consist of Keralites. We need to capitalize and increase our footprint in Kerala to take it to 10 per cent or more of GDP. We have got a few connectivity issues which the government is working on. We should have them resolved quite soon. This opens up easy air connectivity to the Far East and the West. The potential for Kerala's IT opportunities is still unexplored. We have to speed up and for this, we need to increase the availability of supporting infrastructure of the state to bring out the talent that we have inside of us.

Now, transforming our state to become a knowledge economy is key in ensuring that we meet the targets of goals that the state is set to achieve in 2020-2025. And of the visions that I would like to table for 2025 is the vision to make Kerala IT a 10 to15 billion dollar industry in the span of the next 7-10 years. This will directly create 3 lakh or more IT jobs and 15 lakh indirect alternate jobs. For this, the government needs to invest in consolidating existing IT parks and infrastructure around it. We should make it attractive for large investors to come and pick a space like what Andhra Pradesh is doing. We need to support local companies to set up shops and these costs need to be looked at, we need to bring down the cost so that becomes more attractive for people to set up shops here in Kerala. Incentivize industry-academia partnership. We need academic partnershipsto drive innovations. If I look at it, India is a top offshore destination for IT companies across the world and it is just going to grow and the dependency that the world is going to have on India to provide outsourcing is going to grow in the coming years. The industry is expected to grow by 350 billion by 2025. Kerala needs to be a key contributor in this space and for this, we need to transform the state into the best knowledge economy.

To close my remarks for the day, I would like to open up this thought to everybody. The pandemic did not put the IT industry on the back foot. Instead, it has accelerated the need for states like Kerala to wake up and run faster. Thank you.

Part II

Pillars of Knowledge Economy

A. Digital Infrastructure

The Imperatives and Challenges in Building Infrastructure for the Knowledge Economy

S. Somanath

I am really happy to be with all of you and the panelists to chair this session. In building up a knowledge economy for the state, I am really glad that a lot of people are showing enthusiasm. I had the opportunity to listen to all those people in the inaugural session. It has set the ball rolling with regard to what the government is looking for. It is very interesting and I am really happy that we are discussing the infrastructure for knowledge economy in the first session. When we talk about the infrastructure of the knowledge economy, there are many elements to it. In this session, we are talking about two of the important building blocks. The first speaker will deal with the telecommunication networks and the second speaker will deal with the electronics manufacturing activities that the KELTRON stands for.

Infrastructure, however, is not limited to these two areas alone. There is much more in this area. Of course, we can build into it the networks and connectivity, the servers, the storage systems, and the satellite networks that actually can bring about real connectivity. These are all part of the important IT infrastructure. Now, for building IT infrastructure, it is not enough to import a lot of this equipment, assemble them and provide the type of services that we hope to provide. The market is much more in building those ground

---

The author is the Director of Vikram Sarabhai Space Centre. **E-mail:** chairman@isro.gov.in

infrastructures by ourselves in our industries. So we have to look at how the need for this network or the infrastructure will enable the industries to grow. This is one area which we should address.

Similarly, when you want to look at the space-based infrastructure, there is something that is coming up very fast. How can we give the required connectivity directly from the space?This is one area in which we are all interested in looking at the new thought process in providing network connectivity directly from the space routes. When it happens there is another area that is going to develop. Theseare the ground-based data reception systems that the networks and the corresponding equipment are required for those types of nanosystems. In addition, there is a large amount of infrastructure requirements that do not directly deal with IT and IT-enabled services. But there is quite a bit of other establishments that we need to look at when you talk about the infrastructure which was discussed earlier. This is the educational system, the transport network, the services sectors, among others. Now, all of this contributes to building the right type of infrastructure for this knowledge economy to start.

I do not want to make a big talk about it. I only want to point out some points which could be deliberated upon. To begin with, there is a need to look at the investment that is needed in creating such an infrastructure. The question is whether we go ahead and create it incrementallyand then grow it to a bigger size. Another important issue that we need to tag is obsolescence and hence the update that is required for the infrastructure. Is it not enough that you put in place some infrastructure that could be updated periodically? Such an outlook is justified especially because we are dealing with a fast-changing technology. Yet another issue is related to scalability. Of course, you cannot plan a massive network to start with. You start with something, then progressively increase it to cover larger areas and what should be the architecture in such a system? And how do you look at the performance and how do you manage it? So, the technical and organizational structure of this whole system that we are thinking about is something which puzzles me. How do you want to create it on our own, and not merge it with the overall global system? I am sure that the eminent panelists are going to deal with it.

It is not enough that we create all this infrastructure. We should also create the specific knowledge, which is required for serving the whole knowledge society. The creation of knowledge is also requiring its infrastructure. For example, the type of data that you want to create; when the lockdown came, we were short of the lectures that are required to be delivered to students; we were finding it difficult to create the required materials for them. For creating those large amounts of data, which is required for the changing world, we need to look at what is the type of infrastructure needed to create the information or the knowledge itself to serve the needy people. So, these are the points that I want to highlight today and I do not want to elaborate.

Design and Vision of Kerala-Fibre Optic Network (K-FON)

Jayasankar Prasad and *Santhosh Soman*

Kerala government wants to create a knowledge-powered digital society through the digital empowerment of citizens and promote digital lifestyles and e-commerce. This is possible only if we have a proper information infrastructure in place for effective communication, processing, and dissemination of information. The Kerala government has done a study on existing TELCO infrastructure and found that there is only limited fibre infrastructure in rural areas. 4G services in many places are not properly available. The Government/Educational institutions are now getting broadband services from various TSPs.The existing Kerala State Wide Area Network (KSWAN) infrastructure provides connectivity to nearly 3800 offices. KSWAN infrastructure is not scalable to provide connectivity to up to 30,000 institutions. Department of Telecommunications (DoT) has conducted a comparative study concerning broadband density among these high teledensity states and Kerala is not in a back position. In urban areas, we have 92, and in rural areas, 57. This is not sufficient to achieve the vision of the Kerala Government's "Knowledge Powered Digital Society".

One of the main reasons why Kerala is not having proper 4G connectivity across the state is the poor fiberisation of the telecom towers. Nearly 36 per cent of the towers are connected to fiber and the remaining are connected through

Dr. Jayasankar Prasad is the Managing Director of Kerala State Information Technology Infrastructure Ltd. (KSITIL), **E-mail:** jayasankar.prasad@gmail.com and Mr. Santosh Soman is the Implementation Head, BEL. **E-mail:** santhosh.sks@semt.gov.in

microwave which can provide only limited bandwidth (50 to 100Mbps). So fiberisation of all the towers with the existing fiber infrastructure is not possible.

Hence, the Kerala Government has decided to move forward with building a proper fibre infrastructure to bridge the digital divide provide proper connectivity to all government institutions and leverage the infrastructure for TELCOS so that they can deliver proper broadband services in all parts of the state. The main scope of the K-FON project includes the creation of a highly scalable and resilient core fiber infrastructure, provision of high-speed connectivity to 30,000 government institutions, being an infrastructure provider and sharing the infrastructure for TSP/ISP/MSPs.

While designing KFON infrastructure, the main considerations are: (1) Reliability and availability perspective. (2) Optimize the fiber consumption and also optimize the cost and time. Considering these points, KSEB infrastructure has been selected as the platform for laying fiber since KSEB infrastructure reaches most of the areas of the State. Accordingly, it has been decided to lay fiber on KSEB Poles (Transmission and Distribution network) and construct PoPs in KSEB substations, because power failures in substations are very rare. Having decided to lay backbone fiber over the safer transmission line, there is only a remote chance of fiberbeing cut over the transmission line.

To cover the entire geography of the state, it has been decided to go for tiered architecture which includes Tier I (Core), which connects all the districts, Tier II (Aggregation), Tier III (Pre-Aggregation) and Spur for the inter-district connectivity. Also while choosing the technology we had a lot of deliberation on various technologies currently available and conducted workshops with major technology providers. Finally, it was decided to use DWDM technology for the inter-district traffic, IP-MPLS for intra-district traffic and GPON technology for the access network.

Expected outcomes of K-FON include bridging the digital divide by providing free internet to 20 lakh households, leveraging K-FON infrastructure to TSPs on a non-discriminatory basis so that they can provide high-speed broadband connectivity to households in rural areas, providing scalable bandwidth from 10 Mbps to 1 Gbps to the government institutions, depending upon their requirement, providing high-speed connectivity to Start-ups, IT Parks, airports, and Wi-Fi Hotspots. K-FON also provides free access to the e-learning, e-health, and e-governance applications which are hosted at SDC.

5G is the upcoming technology. TSPs are in the final stage of designing and implementation of 5G in India. 5G requires a large number of towers/small cells because it is high-speed connectivity and it is operating at a high frequency.

So we need to have more number of 5G towers/small cells to cover the entire geography. Since we have fiber infrastructure across the state and it is laid over KSEB poles, small cells can be installed on the pole itself. TSP can reduce a lot of CAPEX on 5G Roll out.

With this infrastructure in place, we are expecting many benefits to the citizens which include: (1) Human capital development: Remote delivery of education, job creation, skills enhancements and remote access to health care etc. (2) Infrastructure development: smart cities, smart villages, smart grids and transportation management all can be addressed using KFON infrastructure (3) Infotainment: Proper information sharing and best practices related to e-governance, agri-techniques etc. Also building a platform for delivering services like IPTV, OTT, Content delivery services etc. (4) Innovation will happen with the collaboration of communities like researchers, developers, product development etc. Hence KFON is going to be the key enabler for the knowledge-based economy.

A Vision for Electronics Systems Design and Manufacturing

T.R. Hemalatha

I would like to deliberate on the dream or vision of Kerala State Electronic Development Corporation (KELTRON) and how electronics can thrive in the state because more than manufacturing we are supposed to be an umbrella organization which is to promote other segments of other suppliers in the state.

The demand for electronic goods in general, especially that of mobile phones and computers, is growing exponentially and India is emerging as the second largest market. Of late, in Kerala, there has been an uptick in electronic system and design manufacturing with 268 new units established since 2014. Our Hon'ble Prime Minister said by 2020 India's import bill for electronics will be more than petroleum. I think we are fast approaching that State. If the country is not preparing itself, we are going to find our foreign exchange eroding in a very big way. I think that both the State and the Centre are taking the right steps in identifying drivers and providing encouragement to establish a stable and robust electronic manufacturing eco-system. The rising middle-class population is surely again a driver and improving the infrastructure is important. I also would like to dwell upon the R&D eco-system in the state which is of paramount importance for this industry.

The second is the current challenges of the electronics industry. Ford is shutting down the plants in India for want of microchips. Due to chip shortage,

---

T.R. Hemalatha is the Managing Director of Kerala State Electronics Development Corporation Ltd. **E-mail:** hemalatha@keltron.org

laptop production is getting delayed by five months. This is typically a pandemic situation because the global demand for laptops and mobile phones has gone up and everybody wants to be at home with the classes and work from home. Similarly, the delivery period has increased from 26 to 30 weeks for microchips and power devices.

Expanding Kerala's footprint in electronics, KELTRON, as everybody says was the dream company in India itself during the 1970s and now due to various reasons, it slipped back. The slippage has not been with the KELTRON alone but for the country as a whole. Hence, it is not that the KELTRON alone but the entire country has gone back. In this process why not Kerala's electronics take the lead? This is especially important given the commitment of the government to employ all those who are educated but remain unemployed.

Why does the state not promote the Make in Kerala brand for electronics? It should finally contribute to the economic growth of Kerala. This is especially important because our good talent is going outside the state and outside the country to grab the opportunities. Why not create an R&D and innovation system so that our talent stays here and contributes to the state? There is a lot of potential in all segments of electronics; consumer electronics, industrial electronics, strategic electronics, communication and broadcast electronics, computer hardware and electronic components.

Let's come to the plan and strategy. We can build a good ESDM ecosystem. So, what is this ecosystem? Encourage ESDM start-ups and MSMEs while existing companies are given support from the industry and institutions in Kerala. Build the skill and quality talent pool along with electronic manufacturing clusters by encouraging domestic and FDI funding. Establish three, at least a minimum of two, electronic manufacturing clusters in South, Central and North Kerala. Let us ensure that FDI and major players are invited to the state so they are part of the consumer, components and computer hardware which are going to be in heavy demand. The State can incentivize them so that they come here and give them mass employment which is a key requirement of the state. The MSMEs could be expected to play the feeder role. I have seen 88 new chip design companies located in Bangalore itself. So why not Kerala also have an ecosystem in which big companies establish their R&D and chip design and other electronic design facilities which does not require much infrastructure? This is something that we can really focus on and develop easily.

Then let me come to the manufacturing. Develop three clusters on a focused approach. I say focused because while the requirement of each sector of electronics is specific, the common facilities are almost the same. We could list certain things that may be required here. Then the FDI and other large companies should be incentivized to make additional investments.

Finally, I would like to summarize, stating that this is not impossible, given the right focus we can develop the much-needed manufacturing ecosystem.

Thank you.

Reflections from Experts Across the World

Hideki Esho

Although I am a Kerala lover, my knowledge of Kerala is quite limited. So my remarks on the Budget speech of Dr. Thomas Isaac are quite general.

My first remark is on the object of transforming to a knowledge economy. I should say the final object of transforming the knowledge economy should be placed on an enhancement of the quality of life of the people. In other words, transforming to a knowledge economy is a means of enhancing the quality of life of the people, not the object itself.

My second remark is how to make use of the uniqueness of Kerala society and economy to transform into a knowledge economy. Transforming to a knowledge economy could be attained by making use of the competitive advantages of Kerala, such as the highest literacy rate (93.1%) or the highest human development index (0.779), relatively higher income per capita, low poverty incidence (BPL 7.05% in 2011-12, compared with 21.92% in overall India), gender-bias free society (1,084 female per 1,000 male), and abundance in tourism resources.

Also transforming to a knowledge economy could be attained by making use of the historical, and cultural heritage and uniqueness of Kerala, such as the highest overseas remittance economy (20.7% of NSDP in 2013-14) and the highest per capita consumption economy among Indian states, a high service

Hideki Esho, Professor, Hosei University, Tokyo, Japan. **E-mail:** esho@hosei.ac.jp

sector dependent economy (62.1% of SGVA), and a highly urbanized society (47.7% of the total population of Kerala), higher population ratio of Christians (18.4%) and Muslims (26.6%), and a decentralised government.

Finally, transforming to the knowledge economy could be attained even by making use of the disadvantages of Kerala, such as second highest unemployment ratio and the highest income inequality among Indian states (Kerala's income equality is driven by the super-rich, top 1%), highly dependent on the inflow of migrant labourers from other states especially in the construction sector, the highest labour cost and the lowest population growth rates among Indian states. Kerala is approaching an ageing society preceding other states.

All these things show that Kerala is an exception among Indian states. So I would say all these competitiveness, uniqueness, and disadvantages of Kerala indicate the necessity and inevitability of transforming Kerala into a knowledge economy to further strengthen competitiveness as well as to overcome the weakness. Brand Kerala campaign would be required in a big way to attract foreign as well as domestic investment. Also knowledge economy should be inclusive.

Now, I would like to present some suggestions. Maybe these are already on the agenda or are in progress. The first suggestion is to set up a Kerala platform, which means a collection of open APIs, depending on Aadhaar. The main purpose of this digital platform is to promote innovations of private companies.

My second suggestion is to make use of Non-Resident Keralites, their knowledge, expertise, and savings. It is necessary to create some mechanism to channel overseas remittances to entrepreneurial activities.

The third suggestion is to promote the practical use of ICT knowledge in many fields, not only in medical services, nursing, health care, and education, but also in tourism (including medical tourism, Ayurveda tourism, domestic pilgrimage tourism, Kerala cuisine tourism), food processing (including marine products), and plantation crops (such as cashew, coir, spices, coffee, tea, rubber) where competitive advantages of Kerala lies. The purpose is to upgrade the quality of goods and services to the global standard, which means to realize a «higher quality-higher profit» economy.

And fourth suggestion is to further promote the Kerala start-up mission. Kerala is ranked as one of the top performers in the start-up ranking. Under the banner of KSUM, there are more than 2,200 registered start-ups. However, the presence of IT/ITeS companies is still limited compared with other top performers such as Maharashtra or Karnataka. Availability of funds and skilled workforce remains a challenge. Developing applications corresponding to the smartphone is one of the most promising areas in start-up business. Promoting e-commerce is required. E-commerce has a huge potential to regenerate employment, especially that of women. Women can work from home, which enables them to simultaneously meet the demands of their home and their careers. It creates not only direct employment opportunities, but also creates employment in logistics and warehousing, and also create technology and corporate jobs.

That is all. Thank you very much.

G. Vijayaraghavan

Two interesting presentations, one on connectivity and the second on looking at Kerala as a manufacturing base.

On the connectivity part, it is an interesting proposition. However, the revenue models for K-FON need to be carefully looked at in terms of how to generate revenue for constantly upgrading the obsolescence that technology goes through. It is important to have a clearly defined financing model to make it sustainable without depending on funding from the government. It is also necessary to ensure that the TSPs do not exploit the situation, as the government will most probably be giving the bandwidth at a very reasonable price with the expectation that TSPs will give it free or at a very low cost.

Looking at Kerala as a manufacturing base for electronics, we will need to define a clear policy on the role of the public sector—what they will do and more importantly what the public sector will not do. We will also need to look at the joint sector, where the public sector and private sector come together. We will also need to specify what we expect from the private sector if the project is owned fully by them.

This is important because when it comes to Government business, very often the public sector companies end up competing with the private sector in the state many times selling products manufactured by companies from outside the state which creates an issue by which the private sector or the joint sector is impacted.

G. Vijayaraghavan, Honorary Professor, Gulati Institute of Finance and Taxation.
E-mail: gvrvma@gmail.com

Look at Coconics, a joint venture between KSIDC, KELTRON, UST and a small company associated with Intel. What happened was, in the first major tender itself, you have the public sector competing with the joint sector. So you had partners competing with each other. And the problem there was that the product offered by the public sector was not manufactured in the state. We need to have a clear policy on how we are going to support companies that set up manufacturing units in the state.

Although we have the largest number of start-ups in the country, there is a tendency among them to move out of the state because they believe that there is no ecosystem in the state. Hence, I am happy that the presentation on manufacturing talks about creating an ecosystem. Let us look at China, where you see a lot of small companies and start-ups coming up. A company out of Shanghai, which I visited two years ago, can prepare a design for a product and the product prototype is ready within a day, not in Shanghai, but the manufacturing is happening in Shenzhen, where there are companies that will convert this design within a day into a prototype. For us, anywhere in the country, it will take at least two weeks plus. Ultimately, the prototype comes from China. Many a time if it is to be made in India we have to ensure that we only use certain components, we do not have the facility for quick changes to prototypes.

The other important part of the ecosystem mentioned is the need for quality testing. Here we have a big advantage as we have the Electronic Regional Test Laboratory in Thiruvananthapuram.

What is important is to try to network with the Central Government institutions, the state government institutions and the public sector? Look at some of the university departments thatdo good work the start-up companies. How do we get all of them together and then say, look, this is what the state has and this is what the state lacks today?

There needs to be a big impetus for the start-ups in this area. I see Balagopal on the call. And, you know, the kind of manufacturing, which they were able to do, the quality of the product which came out of the Penpol, now Terumo Penpol, was of the highest international quality.

We need to be clear as to how the state is going to support business here. How do we support companies to get out of the state orbit to get into the national level and how do we then get out of that orbit for the products of the company to be competitive internationally? In the absence of tariff walls, you cannot anymore be manufacturing for Kerala or the Kerala government, you have to be manufacturing for the world and internally competitive, for which the ecosystem is very important.

I conclude by saying that the most important thing is the ease of doing business. I know the government has put in place a system wherein one could start and then get the approvals within three years. I do not think that is going to work because within three years the bureaucrat will find something somewhere and then you are going to be at their mercy and have to pay a ransom. So, we need to look for a clear model by which all approvals come in 30 to 45 days. These are the areas, which I thought I should cover.

Thank you very much.

Raja Rasiah

I shall address a few points about the knowledge economy, and I am sure having been to Kerala many times, a state popularly referred to as God's own Country and, of course, having read Amartya Sen's very articulate book, the Argumentative Indian where he glorifies Kerala, I believe that the structures are there. Quoting what Deepu Zacharia mentioned in the earlier session, 30 per cent of the skilled personnel working in Indian IT firms are from Kerala. Hence, the latent potential is there for hire, provided you can offer the ecosystem that Vijayaraghavan mentioned just now. Now I think even that can be created, but let me just put it in the context of how I have done my research on this topic.

Looking at the proliferation of IR 4.0 technologies, the digital infrastructure required, especially broadband infrastructure, along with the other important instruments like cloud computing and a range of other things that are done in Malaysia, I believe adapting what countries are doing higher in the technology trajectory will help Kerala cheapen and quicken catch up. Malaysia started early in 1999 with smart schools but was overtaken in this area by latecomers, such as Taiwan, Korea and Singapore.

Taiwan and Korea did not just lay broadband digital infrastructure and provide computers with internet support as in Malaysia, but importantly connected and enabled the members of society, including school children with the knowledge nodes in their countries. Listening to Dr. Hemalatha, I see that she has a good idea as to how that can be done in Kerala. I am speaking from meeting hundreds of design engineers I met while giving a public lecture at IIM Bangalore in 2005. Kerala very much has the capability for appropriating synergy

Raja Rasiah, Distinguished Professor, Asia Europe Institute, University of Malaya, Malaysia.
E-mail: rajah@um.edu.my

from that experience and providing the initial incentives to attract a critical mass of such engineers, which should then snowball into a viable IT-supporting community. Connections and coordination between firms, intermediary organizations and related government instruments are very important.

The transformation of Taiwan to embrace robots and drones began intensively in 2017, which even extended to agriculture. They intensified self-sufficiency strategies aggressively from 2017 when Trump declared a trade war with China. Similarly, in manufacturing Trump's trade war forced Taiwanese from selling microchips to Chinese firms, including Huawei. Hence, Taiwan re-shored food-based agriculture and manufacturing well before the COVID-19 pandemic struck. While drones and robots are extensively deployed in farming, manufacturing is increasingly driven by robots in Taiwan. I think you will need to look at why and how they were able to have robots milking cows, ploughing fields, and drones playing a key role in farming. Small farmers and small firms engaged in farming and agriculture in Taiwan remind me of the organization of industrial districts in Italy, though the structures and players are different.

My kind of research requires me to visit the place, I go into the firms and farms and also map the links between all the components of the ecosystem in which they operate, including the incubators in science parks. Instead of completely reinventing the wheel, something we members of the Globelics advocate, we can shorten, cheapen, and simplify the catching-up process by looking at successful organizations higher in the development trajectory. Keralites can and will, of course, create new stocks of knowledge but in a manner where they evolve collectively with adapted knowledge from abroad.

I am confident that this God own loving country will do well to achieve IT integration with positive synergies in the space of little time. I encourage the intelligent leaders of Kerala to visit both successful (e.g. Taiwan and Korea), and not-very-successful (e.g. Malaysia) countries to develop a profound understanding of how effective ecosystems can be planned to support the development of digital infrastructure to appropriate IR4.0 synergies.

Thank you.

Sreejith Nair

Thank youvery much, and Good Afternoon, Dr. Thomas Isaac, Hon'ble Finance Minister, Professor Joseph, and Shri Somanath, the Chairman for the session, Madam Hemalatha, Shri Vijayaraghavan, and all the dignitaries.

I think this is the right time we talk about the Knowledge Economy.

We missed Industrial Revolution I; we missed Industrial Revolution II. We did not miss Industrial Revolution III, but just followed it. Now we are at Industrial Revolution IV. Industrial Revolution IV is signified, or rather defined with the Internet of things, cyber-physical systems, 3-D printing, nanotechnology, biotechnology etc. and devices and systems with unlimited processing power, storage and speed. Kerala could/should position itself to tap the benefits and opportunities in this era and I believe Kerala has all the potential to do so.

So, I just take from where Professor Rajah Rasiah left off and would like to make a comparison between Kerala and Taiwan probably having spent two and half decades in the Far East countries.

Kerala started very well in the early 70s when the legendary Visionary Late Shri KPP Nambiar laid the foundation of an electronic revolution in Kerala and we were way ahead of all of the states in India, and perhaps way ahead of countries like Taiwan. But where are we now?

At the same time in 1974 Hon Hai Precision Industry was started by Terry Gou in Taiwan which later came to be known as Foxconn and as you know has grown into the third largest electronics manufacturer next to Apple and Samsung and a 175 billion US dollar company.

Sreejith Nair, CEO, Coconics Private Limited, India. **E-mail:** sreejith.c@coconics.com

Taiwan and Kerala share a lot of geo-political or rather demographic similarities and just compare Kerala and Taiwan and see the growth both have achieved. We just have to look inward and find out what went wrong or what did they do different from us,

So, this point comes rise to another interesting part, why I believe that Industrial Revolution IV will be suited for Kerala, I believe that in Kerala, we have the DNA of electronics manufacturing systems or as I call it, hardware DNA, and was also coupled with something which is suited for hardware manufacturing or assembly. I like to use the word finger dexterity; which you can find in traditional business-like cashew nut peeling, spinning etc. We have a unique skill of the finger dexterity. We do have an ecosystem. We do have skilled people.

Okay, now we are going to K Economy, we are going to create a large pool of skilled people, and our many technical institutions churn out a lot of skilled manpower. Are we going to just use them only as a Human resource export state? Are we going to remain as a region with four airports and we are going to export this skill abroad or are we interested in creating at least some industry in this state, whereby our people can get jobs?

If the answer is yes. The electronics industry could be the answer to what we are looking for. I say this because, we know that there are many excellent electronic companies already established in the state and of course, KELTRON is there. I can see SFO technology, and somebody is going to make a presentation, and they have one of the best SMT lines in India. We have a few other electronics manufacturing sectors, why cannot all this come under a cluster? To create an ecosystem? I envisage Town or country manufacturing clusters. Like Shanghai or Shenchen. There are huge electronic manufacturing clusters, led by ODM's, Original Design Manufacturers, these are large companies that use the design or what is known as the master reference design given by Technology Corporations and produce, they are not OEMs they are ODM's.

For example, Foxconn the third largest company is not an OEM it is an ODM and it manufactures for some of the big brands like Apple. So, we need to have a concrete step to attract companies like Foxconn, Westron, Pegatron etc. I am sad to say that none of them are seen coming to Kerala like Madam Hemalatha rightfully pointed out that the electronics system design and manufacturing needs to focus. While it is happening in many other parts of the country. So, this is where we have to just sit back and look at what went wrong.

Some years back the multinational companies started the strategy of China Plus One, even before the start of the trade war between the USA and China.

The intention was to have an alternative manufacturing base apart from China due to geo-political equations. And China is no more a country with cheap labour, especially at a skilled level. The process is still being accelerated by US-China trade relations. Far East Countries like Vietnam, Malaysia, Philippines etc. were those to benefit from this move.

My point is, why cannot We Kerala, make a concentrated effort to target at least some of them? Many component manufacturing units in Taiwan that have large facilities in China are on the lookout to relocate or have alternate setups. As we speak now, there is a huge shortage of critical components like LCD display units, in the global market affecting the production of computing machines worldwide. I am pointing out only one of those and there are many such. The Government of India is also coming up with various schemes to attract such investments.

At least a hundred companies have moved out of Taiwan and China. They have moved to Vietnam. They have moved to Malaysia. They have moved to Mexico. They have moved to Thailand and many of them are moving to India. Can we move with concrete steps, and have a clear-cut strategy probably led by K-DISC to attract some of those companies to Kerala?

I strongly believe that Kerala has everything needed to attract these enterprises. A lot of people are coming back to Kerala, NRIs are coming back to Kerala, not only with money, they are coming with skill sets. And these people are willing to work and share their wealth of expertise in the state. So, there is a market which we need to tap. Just to add to what Sri Vijayaraghavan mentioned in his talk, one of the key points of the decision by the Government is to demarcate what the public sector will do and what the Private sector will do.

I will just touch on one point in which the Honourable Chairman asks for investment and scalability. Yes. Taiwan caters to approximately 60 per cent of the production of electronics equipment and if I am not mistaken, Taiwan has only a population of 24 million. The question is demanding aggregation. If an industry has to thrive in Kerala, there has to be a demand aggregation. All industries work on three strategies, you crawl, you walk and you run. So, when you start to crawl that is the nascent stage when the government has to give all support and patronage. The competition is not fair in this world and for the company to have a commercially viable operation; you will take at least three to five years. The first two years you need nurturing from the government. If an industry has to come to a stable state, then you need firm committed nurturing from the government. Number two, you need to make sure that what Mr. Somanath asked about investment. You know, to be very honest to manufacture a plan setup of LCD display does not make a huge investment, but it needs working capital. What is not available in this country is availability and access to easy, affordable Working Capital. I am sure many of my friends who are listening will agree. The young entrepreneurs at the start of the mission, 'all have ideas they have skills, why they cannot scale up, is due to the unavailability of affordable, or rather easily available working capital. So, I would like to request the government and the policy-makers to seriously look at this aspect.

Yes, this is the right time. We have a strong leadership and the Honourable Chief Minister is very clear and determined. He has a vision and he wants to make it happen. The Honourable Finance Minister has a vision he said very clearly in his speech. So, when we aim for our state to have a K-economy, we should also have industries to support the same to some extent at least. In conclusion, I would strongly recommend the Electronic Hardware Industry as the most suitable for our state, you do not need a huge investment, you do not need a big area, and it is not a polluting industry. All that you need is a consensus decision and a strong will to make it happen. I will just conclude by saying that it is the right time now, if not now then when?

Thank you.

Rasigan Maharajh

I want to preface my comments by sharing with you all that I am speaking to you from a continent of approximately 1.4 billion people in the midst of the global COVID-19 pandemic. As I speak, many of the core capitalist economies of world systems and many from the semi-periphery, including Brazil, Russia, India, and China, are preparing their citizens for vaccinations. Africa has neither the vaccines nor the productive capabilities for their production. Whilst we face the gloomy prospect of being left behind or relegated to the back of the queue, we all know that none of us is safe from COVID-19 until all of us are safe. This sad reflection at this time in our contemporary conjuncture provides a useful segue to the comments I want to offer on the presentations by our colleagues on the electronics sector and the knowledge economy.

I want to emphasise the contextual and historical nature of our developmental experiences. I want to challenge the misstatement that suggests the global South missed the first industrial revolution. I would like to raise five main points arising from the presentations by our colleagues. It builds upon the previous pertinent and critical comments already submitted by my fellow eminent panelists. These concerns are: (1) the importance of planning, and development; (2) the essential function of high-quality and ubiquitous public infrastructures; (3) recognising the significance of social shaping of technology and continuously improving the progressive engagement between science and

Rasigan Maharajh, Professor Extraordinary, Centre for Research on Evaluation, Science and Technology, Stellenbosch University, Republic of South Africa.
E-mail: MaharajHR@tut.ac.za

society; (4) redefining and expanding local productive competences within planetary boundaries, and most generally: (5) learning from doing, and doing better through learning.

Firstly, the State of Kerala is universally acclaimed as a strong teacher of developmental praxis. As we venture further into the 21st Century of our Common Era, skills require nurturing and upgrading to meet the technological advances and economic dynamics that inform world systems in our contemporary conjuncture. We, in the global South, look to Kerala to learn more and benefit from the lessons generated in the praxis of state capability improvements through planning.

Secondly, high-quality public infrastructures which are universally accessible and ubiquitous perform an essential function in world systems that are in the main, essentially neoliberal and underpinned by global corruption and the malevolence of private accumulation.

The South African situation starkly contrasts the positive depiction of progress in the Kerala-Fibre Optic Network. We must also learn how to better align our propensity for innovation with the mundane yet crucial requirement of maintaining and upgrading critical public infrastructures. Have we put in place the necessary apparatuses, equipment, and software interfaces to allow and encourage greater utilisation of high-quality public infrastructures, and are these reconciled against our internal demands while advancing our possibilities of enabling autonomous sovereign policy and technological choices based on our revealed realities? Establishing and maintaining critical public good infrastructures such as the fibre network of Kerala must be lauded and protected from the predatory and rent-seeking instincts of private entrepreneurship and the stagnancy of bureaucratic state capture, which maintains the semblance of power whilst disempowering the masses.

Thirdly, in recognising and acknowledging that technologies result from social shaping, we must consistently seek to expand and improve the progressive engagement between science and society.

Fourthly, we must embrace a continuous process of defining and redefining our developmental trajectory to keep within the ecologically defined planetary boundaries while simultaneously seeking the expansion of domestic productive competence. The comparative advantages of Kerala suggested by our fellow panelists reveal a wealth of capacities, capabilities, and competence forged over a long period of development. As Kerala has been a knowledge economy for most of its existence, ramping up the intensity of knowledge production and utilisation suggests even exploring a circular vision even for the digital ecosystem.

Fifthly and finally, Kerala's equitable development history needs to sustain and advance in the current epoch through more learning from doing and by the utilisation of knowledge, doing even better through improving our competencies for shared learning. History has afforded Kerala the brand value of progressive values and this stands the State in a better position than other brand-labels that are unfortunately marred by their respective exploitative praxis. Our localisation of productive capacities, capabilities, and competence offers many more advantages to Kerala and requires further attention and support. We are all proud of Kerala and its developmental pathway. As a guiding light to the global South, we look forward to learning more from you and your experiences. Thank you all again for the opportunity to participate in this significant engagement, and I wish all the best in advancing a better life for all through ICTs.

Thank you.

Richard Heeks

As those in the IT industry are aware, Professor Richard Heeks is the person who wrote the pioneering work on India's software industry. Today, alongside continuing work on India he also focuses on Africa and he's very much a person concerned about industry and harnessing digital technology for development. So, he has sent me a few points which are put up here.

- ***ICTs in education:*** There seems to be a strong emphasis here on distributing laptops. I think what we have clearly learned from the experience of One Laptop Per Child is that "just add laptops" is not going to improve education; indeed, it may do the opposite (unless Covid has forced schooling in Kerala to move to remote learning). Effective e-education should focus on incentivising and resourcing teachers to make more effective use of ICT in their classrooms.
- ***E-Government:*** Has anyone undertaken a proper benchmarking and needs analysis of e-government in Kerala? Where should be the main priorities, e.g. do they lie more in improving public service delivery to businesses, rather than citizens?
- ***Digital Jobs 1:*** The key error made by governments around the world in relation to online digital work from platforms like Upwork and the like is that they provide standard, mass training programmes when what is needed is a much more targeted intervention; focused on individuals who are motivated and capable of undertaking such work, and supporting

---

Richard Heeks, Professor, Manchester University.
E-mail: richard.heeks@manchester.ac.uk

them to build a sufficient online profile that they can then independently bid for work.

- ***Digital Jobs 2:*** I am pleased to see the mention of Kudumbashree given my past work on this. Is there within the plan, an initiative for directing public sector digital tasks to be undertaken by those from more marginalised communities in Kerala?
- ***Digital Jobs 3:*** The private sector could also be brought into this. See e.g. https://timesofindia.indiatimes.com/business/india-business/pandemic-experience-helps-tech-major-capgemini-to-start-hiring-rural-women-in-india/articleshow/79289131.cms
- ***Digital Platforms:*** Digital platforms like Uber, Flipkart etc. have been improving markets and creating jobs across India but the jobs they have been creating often fall below decent work standards. I currently work half-time for the Fairwork Foundation which rates these platforms against decent work standards and engages with them and with policy-makers and other stakeholders to seek to improve those standards. We already operate in India (see https://fair.work/en/ratings/india/) but not in Kerala. If this is an issue of interest to the Kerala government, then Fairwork would be happy to open a dialogue.

Prince Joseph

I believe that the speech by the Honourable Chief Minister and Honourable Finance Minister has laid the background for a digital platform for Kerala. What sparks our interest and catches the signals on our antenna is things like the explicit mention in the State's Budget about Digital Platforms and trying to pave the way for a whole new set of job creations in this area.

Enabled by the understanding of what happened through the pandemic and the '(WFH) work from home', '(WFA)' work from anywhere kind of culture, there is a readiness now for the new normal. This means an excellent commitment to ensuring that the K-FON project goes through seamlessly and the socially ambitious plans, such as the provision of laptops and internet connectivity across the state to all the families that need it. There is a real drive and momentum in this space.

How do we keep that production line running? That disruption forced us to start innovating, to start thinking about how to improve, to think about how to reduce the dependency on some of these risks that we encountered, which will affect our bottom line.

We are now looking very seriously at the industry 4.0 solutions. This is the time to get hyper-connected. So internally, we are a vertically integrated manufacturing company in all senses of the word, for products and processes. Furthermore, now, we want to expand on that, spread out, and become horizontally integrated, linking our supply chain with higher integration and data sharing with our suppliers and our customers. In fact, our approach went

Prince Joseph, Chief Information Officer, SFO Technologies, India.
E-mail: prince.joseph@nestgroup.net

through a couple of iterations and we finalised at the moment on seven streams, which we actually need to focus on for our core business.

We have heard of Foxconn, Keltron and SFO, and they have all had different journeys in the past two and a half decades. The way ahead requires a new set of thinking, capability, skill set, and strategy. There is a need to migrate from a legacy mindset into a growth mindset. What is needed for the future and by our next set of customers is to demonstrate industry 4.0 capabilities.

On exactly what can be reused, optimised, one example is a better view of inventory, across locations, sites, divisions and production stages and utilising this knowledge on material availability to gain benefits. There was a study and analysis that we did, and we came up with a solution that to a good degree of accuracy projected what output we can produce based on the material at hand irrespective of demand. So, how much can we potentially convert at any given point in time?

So a lot of that is gone into Integrations of data systems and tuning of processes. So I was listening to Madam Hemalatha and the plans at Keltron, and I was also thinking, there are some battles. There are some lessons. There are, however, some important steps that we can probably work on at the moment. My focus has always been on trying to ensure that the operations are geared to our customers' needs and most of our target customers are overseas or export-oriented.

Another critical element, I think nobody touched on till now, is cyber security. One of the areas where we need to have a heavy focus is on cyber security as we are stepping more into OT, which is becoming automated and integrated into the IT layers. You cannot do that without having segregation and a good layer of cyber security coming in all these elements. So the investment suddenly on that front has also garnered more weightage.

The helpful fact is that investment in IT and IT projects or technology projects which is going to enable new, lean modern production operations is not hampered; there is recognition of that from all stakeholders. There is an awareness and an appreciation that it is necessary for us to maintain even the position that we have today. And only then can we even imagine or expect to have future growth.

So, I look forward to listening to more of the expert panels. I went through the names, and I thought this was an incredible array of experts weighing in with their inputs from across the globe. I probably do not fit in this elite, academically brilliant panel. So I am really humbled, and these are the thoughts that I just wanted to share. I am happy to take any question or participate in future discussions.

Thank you.

Keun Lee

Actually, I was supposed to be in session one, but I had a meeting with the Council (of Economic Advisors), so I could not join at that time. Now, I am glad to be able to join this last concluding session. As introduced by KJ, I have been recently appointed as the Vice Chairman of Korea's National Economic Advisory Council, which is like the CEA in the USA. Mr. President is the Chairman, and I am the Vice Chairman from this week.

As a policy response to COVID-19, the Korean government has proposed a new policy line called K-New Deal, which has three components. One is the digital infrastructure, the second is the new growth engines, including biotechnology, and the third component is the new social safety deal. So, the government is putting much budget on these three aspects of the new deal.

Today, we have had many discussions about the importance of education and re-skilling and up-skilling in a knowledge-based economy. In this context, one essential issue is making education more accessible, and an e-learning system by digital technology is one of the most efficient means to achieve this. You can make education not only efficient but also based on mass customization. Another thing is the digital labour market. Now-a-days, many web or app-based services are matching between tasks and people supplying that task or service.

Another topic we can discuss is about start-ups and entrepreneurship. Every country tends to have its policies for start-ups, and we may learn from experience in China or Thailand. They are creating something like start-up centres or spaces

Keun Lee, Director, Centre for Economic Catch-up, Seoul National University, South Korea & Vice Chairman, Presidents Economic Advisory Council.
E-mail: kenneth@snu.ac.kr

where they supply potential entrepreneurs with basic devices like 3D printing machines, laser cutters, and other basic devices for new entrepreneurs.

In the meantime, when we talk about a knowledge-based economy, it is often useful to distinguish two types of knowledge, namely scientific knowledge (represented by academic articles) and technological knowledge (often represented by patents etc.). Then, a related issue is how to translate them into practical usages by industries, namely the issue of commercialization. Without an effective national innovation system, scientific knowledge tends not to be utilized but remains within the ivory tower.

Last, to be effective in policy-making and implementation, one simple but effective approach is benchmarking preceding success stories from neighbouring countries. In this regard, I would say China might be an obvious benchmark case for India to derive and take some lessons. As is well-known, many policies in Korea used Japan as a benchmark, which is a cost-effective way.

B. Innovation System

On the Knowledge System

M.S. Rajashree

I am extremely happy to participate in this international consultation on transforming Kerala into a knowledge economy. I feel privileged to chair this session dealing with the innovation system, the fundamental pillar of a knowledge economy. The need to innovate is the basic prerequisite of a knowledge economy. Kerala has a history of chartering an innovation system centred around its people. Education and health were the primary emphases for development. Along with public funds, private funds were also channelled for affordable health care and education, thus making Kerala a development model in these sectors for the rest of the country.

Innovation and technological changes are the key drivers of the knowledge economy. In order to leverage these two elements Kerala needs to develop an ecosystem based on an efficient knowledge system. A knowledge system that connects industry, education, research institutions, and government is a critical element in contributing to regional and local innovation systems. The efficiency of this knowledge system is predominantly determined by how well the knowledge is organized to contribute towards development at the local and regional levels. Once the industry is enabled to use the knowledge created from education and research the industry will be able to offer knowledge-intensive businesses and service activities. Studies have shown that manufacturing industries, especially MSMEs, are becoming increasingly innovative with higher R&D expenditure and greater integration with knowledge providers, viz educational institutions and R&D centres.

M.S. Rajashree, Vice Chancellor, APJ Abdul Kalam Technological University, Kerala.
E-mail: vc@ktu.edu.in

Knowledge Systems can be strengthened by creating a common infrastructure and developing missions/entities responsible for facilitating greater connections between components of the Knowledge System. Kerala has demonstrated this by establishing the Kerala Start-up Mission (KSUM) and the Kerala Development Innovation and Strategy Council (K-DISC). KSUM has developed a vibrant start-up ecosystem in the state. The state has initiated a start-up movement through the KSUM for forging and implementing forward-looking startup-related policies. KSUM supports the start-ups through a plethora of activities for strengthening them in the state through infrastructure, funding, linking start-ups to businesses, and providing all other support services. The present focus is to foster the growth of innovation-led technology start-ups. Kerala possesses a unique model of connecting academics, industries, R&D institutions, and start-ups through the KSUM. KSUM is also responsible for the setting up of major infrastructure facilities and other allied services necessary for start-ups. The facility thus set up is shared by all the stakeholders across the state.

Kerala Development Innovation and Strategy Council is a strategic think-tank and advisory body by the Government of Kerala. K-DISC brings out strategic plans, identifies new directions in technology and creates a conducive ecosystem in Kerala for fostering innovations through various engagements with academia, research and development organizations and the government.

In the knowledge economy, research priorities and policy issues should be explored by a group of institutions that form part of the knowledge system. 'Knowledge' as a concept should be unfolded into elements that can be analyzed and applied to both industry and regional innovation. Fundamental research is needed to understand how knowledge is transforming innovation processes and enabling sustained economic development. The outcome of this research will lead to improving all the components that are part of the knowledge system. This will lead to the understanding of new interventions required in furthering developments of the economy through infrastructure creation, policy-making etc.

The competencies required for driving innovation and embracing technological advancements towards the development of all sectors require a robust Higher Education System. The Higher Education system should: (i) enable the creation of talents with an innovation mindset; (ii) produce an agile workforce with competencies in digital technologies; (iii) lay emphasis on IP-based research; (iv) facilitate strong industry connections; (v) generate entrepreneurs capable of creating businesses which can bring in sustainable economic development with access to national and international markets. I hope these issues will be taken up in the next session.

Industry 4.0 is transforming the way businesses work and also the manufacturing landscape as a whole. Adoption of digital technology in all sectors, empowering such sectors, will be a game changer in Kerala's journey towards a Knowledge Economy. In this effort, Inclusive development can be made possible if the digital divide is properly addressed. Kerala's proposed infrastructure for connectivity will address this. Traditional manufacturing technology will be accelerated by Industry 4.0 technologies such as intelligent robots, autonomous drones, sensors, and 3D printing, which are proven to be exponentially growing technologies. The convergence of these digital technologies and existing industries will have a positive impact on the local and global value chain. The innovation activities around these converged areas will need to be channeled to the global innovation system thus creating an open innovation culture in Kerala.

An open innovation ecosystem that is connected to a global innovation system, especially in high technology areas, will be a promising base for Kerala's growth and development based on the Knowledge Economy. Such a vibrant ecosystem will reinvent itself with the dynamics of each of its components and reorganize the organization of knowledge and its flow in the value chain from time to time for the state's economic development.

Evolving an Innovation Ecosystem for Kerala

P.V. Unnikrishnan

I shall start off with some brief comments on the Kerala Development and Innovation Strategy Council (K-DISC). It is a relatively new organisation initiated in the state in 2018. It is only one of its kind because State Innovation Councils established at the instance of Sam Pitroda in 2010 in all other states have been wound up throughout the country. The only state with the remnants of the State Innovation Council is Kerala, where it has been remodelled. That is how K-DISC originated. Dr. K.M. Abraham, our founder Chairman, has already made a brief introduction about K-DISC activities. Hence, I will not attempt to make a comprehensive overview of K-DISC activities.

To give a taste of the activities leading to innovation promotion in government done by K-DISC, I will touch upon three projects: a project called the Blood Bag traceability, where we work with the General Hospital and the Parasalla Community Health Centre. They work in a hub and spoke mode to meet blood transfusion needs. In this project, we have used a technology developed by Bagmo Private Limited, a start-up in Maker Village to reduce the perishability of blood bags using IoT devices. The second one is a collision avoidance pilot with Intel for KSRTC wherein, using telematics, the possibilities of collision between vehicles are reduced. This will be implemented in new vehicles for KSRTC financed by KIIFB. The third one is a real-time retinal image

---

Dr. P.V. Unnikrishnan is strategic advisor, K-DISC. **E-mail:** ms.kdisc@kdisc.kerala.gov.in

quality assessment and feedback system for the Government Ophthalmological Hospital, Trivandrum. This is done with the support of C-DAC. These projects undertaken by us belong to Industry 4.0 technology adaptation in government departments.

My focus, however, is on the innovation ecosystem, which is primarily for democratizing the innovation system in the state. It is a flagship programme of K-DISC. The objective of this programme is basically to nurture young talents interested in pursuing avant-garde research academics and business model building. We have promised a three-year handholding for idea creation, prototyping, testing, and launching. Prominence is also given to social innovation, along with business development. We partner with the Start-up Mission. Capacity Building of mentees is around the Stanford University Methodology of design thinking, which has now become the *de-facto* standard for real-life problem-solving. We have a programme for mentoring mentors specially developed for us by the IIM, Calicut. This looks at a new product development framework integrated with a fuzzy front-end. Basically, we are trying to draw practices from the industry for product development, trying to weed out the fuzziness of the ideas and to put the process in the discipline of new product development.

We have a programme in which any new innovation can be fostered with its focus on democratising innovation, it cannot be a blueprint programme. It has been continuously evolving. Over the years, there has been an increase in the number of ideas that came up; 1391 ideas in the first year (2018) which increased to 2000 during the second year and almost doubled that in the third year. We have a very strong funnelling approach to removing ideas that might not work and that are not worth pursuing. Thus, we had to reduce the ideas in 2018 to 204 which increased to 371 in the second year and 800 in the third year. We have put in a mechanism for generating ideas from schools, colleges and universities. We have a network of 1143 institutions during 2018 we just now enhanced this to 2900. Around 400 of them in our network are professional colleges and university departments and the rest of them are schools, polytechnics and other institutions. From each of these institutions we have, two facilitators who are our ambassadors who have been trained in the industry 4.0 and the innovation methodology. We have tried working out a hub and spoke mechanism wherein eventually the hubs would emerge as Centers of Excellence. This would be linked to various partner institutions making the spoke mechanism. We have developed a very clear methodology not only for screening the ideas, but also for improving the group dynamics within the ideas through group techniques.

This is the architecture of the young innovation programme which we have built up. We have a completely electronic platform for doing all our operations. We have a digital idea platform, which is connected to high schools' polytechnics, higher education institutions and research centres. We have District Innovation Councils, which are going to come into action from this year onwards in the evaluation programmes. We also have a mentor-mentee platform, which is completely electronic. One of the very important things that we have found as a part of the first few years of the programme is that very systematic mentoring is required, both from the industry experts as well as from the academia for translating ideas to clear targets. We have not been able to put that in place during the first year. But during the second year, we have been able to put in place an electronic platform for this. We hope that the quality of delivery would substantively relate to mentoring. The mentors have been trained and positioned.

One of the weaknesses of the programme is that we do not really get good ideas. Essentially, people pick up ideas from Google and these are not really real-life ideas. So we have brought into two methodologies, one a methodology of creating real-life problem statements with the help of practitioners through community practices. This is an internationally renowned methodology of situated cognition. Secondly, we are trying to create a process of innovation sandbox, which is a methodology of improving the real-life, real-time, problem-solving experience using crowd-sourcing and open innovation and bringing in vital user experience.

Now, thanks to the efforts of the Honorable Finance Minister, who has made an evaluation of the programme. He wanted us to scale up this programme substantively, and we are restructuring YIP in 2021 to meet his dream. YIP is a mix of challenges. Right now, following the idea challenge, we have accelerated the innovation track. But beyond that, we are also now bringing in team-based hackathons and a coordinated programme of rapid proto-typing jointly with fab-lab and start-up mission. With this, we are hoping that the Young Innovation Programme is going to make a major transformation.

The outcome so far is that 31 products have been structured for priority funding, and we could hardly spend 1 million rupees for this process. That is one of the limitations of the programmes. We have been able to do the democratization reach out to the campus, bringing together the teaching Community and the students, but in terms of converting the ideas into innovations, we are lacking, and that is why we want to get into a sandbox methodology for deepening the innovation process.

Now, coming to the next programme which caters to ecosystem building in the MSME sector. In the One District One Idea Programme, we have identified 266 clusters throughout the state. It covers Handicraft Handloom Kudumbasree Service clusters, Kerala Bureau of Industrial Promotion Manufacturing clusters, and other manufacturing clusters. These have been selected for a challenge. Digital University has come up with an excellent training programme for the core group. We have brought in professors from the commerce department, economics department and also from engineering college to work in the field with these clusters and develop innovative action plans for them. Thus, we are bringing in academia in a big way to work with the industry to solve their problems—Making the triple helix model a reality. The objective is to come up, not with incremental growth as the Honourable Minister was discussing in the previous session. We are focused on not incremental growth but exponentially growing clusters, i.e. innovation clusters.

Now, coming to the one local government one idea programme. The design of the programme is similar. We start off with a shelf of projects that local governments have identified, run hackathons across specific domain sectors, go to a local government marketplace, select products for support and then these go back to the local government for implementation.

And the last programme is the local innovation programme. The design of the programme is as follows. We crowdsource ideas from anyone capable and interested. There is a panel of experts at the State and District levels. There is a rating scheme based on which we come up with a local marketplace for the POC and the pilot, which will be taken up through various local governments and the public sector. One of the most important things is that the first product that K-DISC has initiated is ready to get into manufacturing. Rajeesh Rajan, a Polytechnic diploma-holder had developed a ragas engine—A two-stroke elliptical IC engine. We had sent his design for computer fluid dynamics studies. And basically, this has helped him improve and patent the engine. He wants to take it up to the aircraft engine manufacturers and to work with DRDO. Yesterday he came and presented that to us. And so, the local innovation promotion programme, which we kicked off three years back, has just started bearing fruits.

Let me conclude by talking about the three pillars of focus in the budget. One is the Innovation Economy, the Digital Transformation and Creating new workforce. The innovation economy component is the one that I talked about primarily. I also briefly touched upon digital transformation, because the ODOI programme looks at the digital transformation of MSMEs. The local government's'One-idea-one-Local-Government programme' also takes up digital transformation. We have been involved in a small scale in developing the new knowledge economy workforce. We have been working with KBA and ICT Academy to develop the Accelerated Blockchain Competency Development Programme. Now the new knowledge worker's skilling programme has been also passed on to us. So, this is a great opportunity for K-DISC along with its partners to have been involved in the three pillars, so our final objective would be essentially to involve with the Kerala Knowledge Economy building process through skilling of knowledge workers, driving innovation ecosystem, innovation collectives and start-ups and also moving towards digital transformation of various sectors.

Last but not the least, let me touch upon the very critical point that Professor Lundvall had raised in the first session—if we focus only on scaling the Knowledge Workforce and strengthening the ICT industry, there is a possibility of alienation from a section of the non-digital economy. A massive section of the citizenry will be left out of the knowledge revolution. It is a very important point. Through the higher education strengthening, digital transformation, innovation building programme, as well as the Social Security initiatives we have looked at this in totality in the budget. I would like to congratulate the Honourable Finance Minister for coming up with such an excellent blueprint for the Kerala Knowledge Economy.

Thank you.

Kerala Start-up Ecosystem

Tom Thomas

We are always leading the way. In 2019, we launched one of the largest start-ups in the country with a 1.80 lakh sq. feet area. In 2016, the policy came on, and the objective was to create organizations that create jobs and wealth. Kerala, unfortunately, have a huge brain drain that comes in terms of qualified people moving for job as well as good start-ups moving out of the state looking for a larger market. We have been trying to solve this: how do we attract the talent back? How do we create more talent that is really aligned with the new knowledge economy? How do we inspire people to take newer technologies? To address these questions, the first is to kind of evangelize about technology and startup. The second is to create programmes that make use of new technology and this includes digital fabrication, blockchain, augmented reality,virtual reality etc.

Then how do we ensure a good talent pool is being developed? So, we work a lot with KTU and other universities to make this happen. How can we encourage youngsters and professionals to start building solutions? We do a bunch of challenges; we create innovation zones and may try to make sure that there is always something new happening in the ecosystem. One week of the supporting experiment, then grow into start-up and that is the way we have launched. We help them get into the incubator and give away the early-stage funding so that they have a launch pad.

Mr. Tom Thomas is the Project Director, Kerala Start-up Mission.
E-mail: tom@startupmission.in

Finally, we look at how we help them to work with the government. How do we make sure that there is a large capital available for the start-ups to grow? In terms of the evangelization part, we have four flagship conferences around the year; one focuses on student summits. Then, we ensure that more women take up entrepreneurship. We have also formulated the women's free-lancer development programme, where we are trying to find women who have left jobs due to various family circumstances and would like to get back. How can they have the flexibility to work from home and thus contribute to economic growth?

The second part is the educated; primarily what we have done here is set up a network of 200 plus innovation cells in various academic institutions—this helped buy those small breakthrough ideas from these colleges. Maybe a student who is good in technology and we tried to get them into other programmes like FAB Academy summer school for the various universities across the world. The FAB academy programmes are very important. The reason is we are considered one of the top two centres across the world to run this programme, and so far had about 60 graduates, and all of them were placed in good companies, many of them working with hardware start-ups to build their own product. This programme is possible because we have a large network of state-of-the-art fabrication labs. We have two main labs in Kochi and Thiruvananthapuram. We have 20 smaller labs across the state. This essentially gives students and youngsters access to new technologies like 3D printing, laser cutting etc. We can really allow students to build and that is an essential part of both learning as well as creating newer companies. What we have recently done is work with MIT to set up a super fab lab. So this is the MIT fabrication lab duplicated here. The journey of the fab lab is the kind of a long journey. What we have also realized is that there are other newer technologies that we need to look at.

Unfortunately, Covid came in, and we had to step back and see how we could offer online. Here, we give access to advanced machines, gadgets and learning capabilities. This also gives access to high-powered GPU and the provider is that of mentoring and training programme or started working on these future technologies. Going forward, this is where we really need to be, because if you look at the state, you have a favourite of software coming up. We are starting to be known as the start-up hub, but that is not enough from our perspective. We need to be known as the hub for one of those technologies so that we can attract talent interested in those technologies and start-ups based on it.

What we also do with the various government departments is to create innovation zones. For example, we worked with the Water Authority to find out some of the solutions to their problems. We do this by running various idea challenges, throwing out problem statements and finding good ideas that can be developed. For the products and ideas that come up, we have specialist incubators that take them in and help them finish engineering prototypes and go to the market. We have one for hardwareand bio-technology. We also have one that will take mobile-based technologies which give launch Space Technology incubator in Thiruvananthapuram. This is in collaboration with ISRO so that we get access to the technology and products of ISRO. In addition to this, we have our own incubators across five cities in the state, all of which provide mentorship and various networking opportunities for start-ups. What we have started doing additionally is to link them with industries so that they get good, early adopters and good business.

We also provide early-stage grants through innovation grants, seed loans, patent support, and R&D grants for companies. In addition to this, we provide marketing support. We used to take them outside India for various conferences, and that has been a really good platform for many start-ups to learn global business.

We have also created a venture fund, with the support of the government. So far, about Rs. 74 crore of funding that our start-up can have access to, and for that we work with a variety of leading partners across the world. It is very easy for departments to procure from various start-ups at the tender process. Through this, up to Rs. 1 crore of product can be purchased by departments from the state. Some of those key projects are also being handled by K-DISC. Today, we have about 2.6 lakh sq.feet of incubation space spread across the state.

We are probably the only state that has incubation space available throughout the state. Other states have a concentration in one city like Bengaluru or Hyderabad. Kerala is making sure that start-ups across the state have access to information space and mentoring. We have about 1463 start-ups, and for them the support of Rs. 50 crore of funding is available. Last year, we launched the integrated start-up complex, which is 1.8 lakh sq. feet building. The key question for us now is how do we get start-ups in, how do we create newer technologies? How do we get them enough skill and talent? If we can find some of those key opportunities and build around them, this would attract larger companies to the state.

Reflections from Experts Across the World

Xiaolan Fu

The first presentation gave a comprehensive introduction to the various programmes introduced in Kerala that included, among others, the Young Innovators Programme of the K-DISC, One District One Idea, and the Local Government programme. I am really impressed to see that you are doing all the right things. Kerala may become another star in India like India has Bangalore. I think Kerala will be another star in the fourth Industrial Revolution. All the technologies for the future and the start-up ecosystem are set in place.

India's economy has taken off since the 1990s. It is really going very fast, and India now is one of the emerging countries. I believe that India will continue to grow very fast. India has many world-class minds and has not reaped the potential. I have been thinking about how to help in this aspect. Here, one of the significant aspects is the implementation of the great plans. The implementation issue is not confined only to the innovation or science and technology sector. We need the right institutional, economic, and political background to enable all these bright plans to deliver.

These are excellent plans, but they are very much focused on domestic activities in India. My research about innovation in China explains why China has been able to catch up. One of the lessons that we could learn from China is the role of an open national innovation system. In my book, China's Path to

---

Xiaolan Fu, Director, Technology and Management for Development Centre, University of Oxford, England. **E-mail:** xiaolan.fu@qeh.ox.ac.uk

Innovation, I described that the Chinese national innovation system is linked with the global innovation system and global knowledge pool through various links such as international trade, foreign direct investment, and both. You are aware that India is becoming an attractive destination for MNCs, and Indian MNCs are increasingly investing in other countries.

We could observe the active involvement of Indians in some of the significant innovating countries and building their national innovation system. The movement of people facilitates this. Such mobility of people facilitates the exchange of ideas, especially the tacit knowledge that otherwise rarely crosses the borders. Then, looking at China's experience in trade, it is evident that China has the highest level of trade-to-GDP ratio among major developing countries, and it is higher than Japan and the US. China is the largest recipient of foreign direct investment and has become a significant investor abroad in recent years. Further, China has also benefited from diasporas exchange in recent years.

I think India's experience is the same; during the early years, there was much worry about brain drain, which is now increasingly being brain circulation. It is also correctly used to teach the technology to accelerate knowledge exchange and innovation. Another key factor is international collaboration. Now, countries are increasingly using international collaboration to foster innovation. This is not only for developing countries to stay where they are. They want to collaborate with the advanced industrialized countries for innovation. Industrialized countries like the OECD, the European Union, and the US very much emphasize collaborative innovation, and my research, which was published last year, also finds that Chinese firms benefit from innovation collaboration. So, this kind of open national innovation system in China uses both domestic and international resources, talents, and markets. There are two major drivers in this process. One driver is the market, and another driver is the State, although they have different roles. The role, however, changes at different stages of innovation. The State, in the early stage, plays a more important role in heavy investment and high-risk activities, and that of the market is more at the lower end of commercialization. So, I think this open national innovation system approach could be considered in Kerala.

In the UK and in many of the other innovative countries, Indian scientists are excellent. They are good in science and management and have a leading role in technology companies. I think the start-up ecosystem design is also brilliant. However, bringing the international dimension and putting it in a broad context is also important. I think that the support needs to come from the whole country, especially the industrial foundation, and infrastructure, to make it really deliver its full potential.

C. Balagopal

I want to specifically talk about one aspect, which is from the perspective of the high-tech manufacturing industry operating in Kerala. More specifically, what kind of support and what kind of synergistic role can the state play in the innovation ecosystem? I think the biggest user of all the innovative science and technology products and facilities that are sought to be created by K-DISC and by the Kerala Start-up Mission is going to be the MSMEs. I have been associated with the Start-up Mission right from its very beginning, and I am impressed at the progress that has been made, but I think we are losing something by this almost exclusive focus on start-ups. As I said earlier, the biggest user of know-how and innovation will be the existing high-tech manufacturing industry. There is a saying in innovation that necessity is the mother of invention! So somebody must be feeling the pressure. Somebody must be feeling a problem burning a hole in their balance sheet, so much so that they are always seeking a solution. That burning 'necessity' to innovate can never come from a young guy studying in college or someone who may have some idea.

The second thing is the ability to recognize the value of innovation as a property of business and industry. Only when you are looking for something, you will be able to identify what you are seeing. So, the problem here is we have a dichotomy. We have R&D centres and high-tech laboratories of research institutions that are working on projects; somewhere else, we have industry, which has problems. And the two are not talking to each other, not meeting to discuss these problems. So I recommend that both K-DISC and Kerala Start-up Mission create such a platform to bring industry and institutes together.

C. Balagopal, Founder and Former Managing Director, Terumo Penpol Ltd.
E-mail: cbalagopal@gmail.com

I am talking from first-hand experience because I set up a small start-up that grew globally before I sold it as the World's largest maker of high-quality blood bag systems. I had the great sense to develop a personal excellent working relationship with Sree Chithira Tirunal Institute research laboratories. I also used the Keltron tool room, which today houses GIFT. I used the facilities and expertise of the Indian Institute of Science, Bengaluru, and several other top R&D establishments. So I think what is very important is that the platform must be created that will enable MSMEs that are already successfully working within Kerala to be able to access and continuously have interaction with research institutions, research laboratories, and even the Maker Spaces, Maker Village and all the other facilities.

The second proposal, which I have, is related to the first one. These MSMEs include companies with revenue up to Rs. 2,000 crore and are globally successful, with huge balance sheets, operating in diverse areas ranging from steel casting, medical device manufacturing, electronics hardware, medical diagnostics, dental prostheses etc. Now, here, you can have a system of internships, fellowships, and sponsored projects for which K-DISC can again provide the platform. These industries will be pleased to welcome bright young students from engineering colleges and science research laboratories to go to their facilities to work on their projects and learn by working on the shop floor with their scientists and technologists. Similarly, young technologists from industry can go to R&D institutes and do such programmes. Unfortunately, today they are all working in silos.

Third, if you take the successful high-tech manufacturing sector already operating in Kerala, they can be grouped into specific, contiguous clusters. And there are natural clusters already existing: you can have a medical device cluster around Thiruvanthapuram based on TPPL, HLL, and TTK Healthcare; a steel casting product cluster like PeeKay Steel Castings around Calicut; spice extracts and food processing cluster at Kozhencherry, and then a garment cluster at Kizhakkambalam. If you create these clusters, then I think that would enable some common facilities to come up, which K-DISC can provide, which will be beneficial to these clusters since it will be difficult for an MSME to set up a laboratory or a testing facility.

To sum up, many elements of science, technology, and innovation ecosystems already exist here. The point is to connect the dots. So you have elements of a beautiful start-up ecosystem, you have very successful high-tech companies, you have one of Asia's premier research institutes in Thiruvanthapuram for medical devices, and so many others in other advanced fields if you can create a platform for them all to talk to each other and exchange ideas, you will find a tremendous amount of cross-fertilization of ideas happening which will lead to very good things.

Thank you.

Erika Kraemer-Mbula

It is really fascinating to hear and learn about Kerala's experience. It has also allowed me to reflect on the environment in South Africa. It also helps to think about our own ecosystems and highlight how important it is to collaborate and share experiences.

I was happy to listen to the presentations about the innovation ecosystem. Two initial presentations spurred the discussion, and it appears that the State has done a lot in pioneering to support the start-ups at various levels. I can see from the presentations that there is quite a good and deep understanding that supports the local innovation system, not only about creating incubators and accelerators but also requires a broad understanding of the resources and the actors at different levels that they are and also have an in-depth and real-time understanding of the challenges affecting the business community and the local entrepreneurs. I think this has become very evident in the time of COVID. I just had a quick look at the news, which shows that the support for entrepreneurs has been quite intensive during the pandemic in Kerala.

I would like to make three points, some of which have been raised by the previous commentators. The first point relates to the period of the commitment that we need to build a local innovation ecosystem. Supporting an innovation ecosystem is not a once-off initiative. It requires a long-term commitment and is quite challenging when the conditions change. The sustainability of this effort

---

Erika Kraemer-Mbula, DST/NRF/Newton Fund Trilateral Chair in Transformative Innovation, the 4IR and Sustainable Development, South Africa, and Vice President, Globelics. **E-mail:** erikakm@uj.ac.za

is also being raised by others that have to do with implementation. I would like to emphasize here that for local ecosystems to be sustainable in the long run and survive the changes over time in terms of prioritization and financial resources, it is important to empower not only the local businesses but also the whole constellation of organizations and actors that is around. This includes entrepreneurial centres, training organizations, chambers of commerce, NGOs, tech communities, centres of institutional research, providers of funding, and so on. The empowering and supporting of these organizations is essential because they will carry the load and fulfil the functions needed for a local ecosystem to thrive and survive, even in the absence or in cases where government support may be weaker than others.

I think from my point of view, there is a very important role that government can play in empowering the constellation of actors that surround firms. Another important role that government can play, as raised by others, is to guide the direction of this local innovation ecosystem. So, a lot has been discussed about the outcome. Preserving the quality of natural and social ecosystems must be part and parcel of how innovation systems are conceptualized, supported, and maintained. Others have talked about environmental sustainability as the natural environment, and society can be seen as resources and as part of the outcomes. So, do we maximize profit only for firms? Or do we also maximize profit for the environment and society? Here, we bring up all dimensions of inclusion, and this is a point that I would like to reflect on the context in which I am.

We often talk about the need to create entrepreneurs, and I usually sit uncomfortable when I hear that expression. Because, I only need to step out of my house and go and buy bread, and I walk past at least 20-30 entrepreneurs. Many of them are informal, and many of them are survivalists, but some others are testing and trying new ideas. And we often leave these actors out of how we think about entrepreneurs in local innovation systems. And again, I think there is a lot of room to think about how we bring in these new and emerging technologies, including digital technologies but also more advanced ones that we are referring to here. This large pool of entrepreneurial resources that we have in our context as a formal economy brings us ideas about how to make our local innovation systems more inclusive and how to think about upscaling, reproducing, and so on—some of these businesses and connecting them more successfully with their new and emerging technologies.

The final point that I want to make again is a stronger rooting of our local innovation systems with the reality that we live in, in the sense of connecting to the informal economy and bringing that inclusion into it. I do not think there is a contradiction between supporting and routine local innovation systems with the global dynamics. I think there is a lot that can be gained in terms of exchanging ideas. I see a lot of room for South-South collaboration for the fusion of ideas and social innovations. There is quite a lot of similarity and a lot of room to share and to learn, and embedding these dynamics in how we conceptualize and support local innovation systems is also very important. I am going to stop there.

Thank you.

Srikumar Chattopadhyay

Introduction

The Kerala Budget 2021-22 (Thomas Isaac, 2021), an innovative, audacious, and inspiring budget, proposed Kerala's development leap to a knowledge-based economy and knowledge society. Ecological sustainability has an important role in this journey. Kerala's achievements in the social sector have met most of the criteria envisaged under social sustainability. However, on the ecological front, there are perceptible gaps that warrant due attention in the course of transiting to the knowledge society. In this chapter, we intend to deal with natural resource management, one of the core components of ecological sustainability.

The natural resource base provides the foundation for economic development. The nature and type of resource use change with the progress of civilization and technological advancement. Production of knowledge, which began with the settled agriculture and surplus production of food, witnessed tremendous growth during the history of human civilization that progressed through the agricultural and industrial revolutions and now entered the era of the knowledge revolution. The social, cultural, economic, and ecological orders of the World are changing with the production of knowledge and its useful application. The transformation is from a resource-intensive society to

Srikumar Chattopadhyay, ICSSR National Fellow, GIFT. **E-mail:** srikumarc53@gmail.com a knowledge-intensive society that is deeply innovative, dependent on the use of human knowledge, sensitive to natural and environmental resource use, and ecological resilience. Formation of human capital, precision management, efficient resource use, multi-level decision-making, and new knowledge generation are integral part of the knowledge society.

Propositional and Prescriptive Knowledge

Kerala is blessed with strong natural resource endowments. The State has successfully harnessed the traditional natural resources, including hydropower generation. However, the management of natural resources is not always prudent. There is a complex ecological interdependence among the components of natural resources. A linear approach often fails to take into account this complexity. As a result, several problems crop up, and ecosystem services are jeopardized. The change that is taking place with respect to natural resource use or natural capital in Kerala warrants proper attention to improve the knowledge base. Joel Mokyr (2002), in his '*The Gifts of Athena*,' proposed two types of useful knowledge: propositional knowledge and prescriptive knowledge. Propositional knowledge focuses on how nature works, and prescriptive knowledge focuses on the use of techniques. The trajectory of the natural resources-based economic development in several countries underscores the importance of combining useful knowledge with strategies to develop capabilities to transfer technology and knowledge from other (leading) economies, as well as local scientific organizations relevant to promoting natural resource-based industries (Ville & Wicken, 2015). The close interaction of scientists to solve specific problems of local industry is found helpful in several countries. Kerala has to evolve this practice for its future development initiatives.

Some Suggested Sectors of Action in Kerala

It is important for Kerala to examine the present use of natural resources and reorient present practices, wherever necessary, for contributing to the knowledge economy. Here, we attempt to briefly indicate some of the sectors to initiate actions.

Bridging the Knowledge Gap in Existing Natural Resource use Sectors

Bridging the knowledge gap assumes great significance in pursuing a natural resource-based knowledge economy. For example, to site a seaport, it is important to search for a coastal stretch that is neither accreting nor eroding. Accretion and erosion along the coastline are related to sediment movement. The sediment transport pattern along the Kerala coast varies temporally and spatially. Some parts of the Kerala coast experience domination of net northerly drift, whereas in some cases, the movement is southerly. Although there are some studies, site-specific knowledge is lacking in many cases. The impact of climate change and consequent sea-level rise will further complicate the prevailing situation. It is important to generate a detailed knowledge base to suggest appropriate locations for the siting of ports, particularly fishing ports. Otherwise, the port may be affected and will need huge investment to keep it operational.

Kerala is well endowed with heavy minerals such as beach placer deposits. These deposits are available both inland at some depth and also offshore. Extraction of beach placer deposits induces coastal erosion. How will a balance be achieved in this case? Excavation of inland deposits calls for relocating settlements, which is a big challenge given the population distribution in Kerala. There is scope for technology development and planning initiatives to consolidate settlements.

The State is facing the problem of harnessing blue water. Watershed management and river/stream renovation are increasing the potential for blue water availability. However, there is little initiative in controlling stormwater flow. Production of stormwater is increasing with growing urbanization and expansion of built-up areas. Management of stormwater is a big challenge. Greywater management is another sector. The reuse of greywater and stormwater is a priority sector. Many countries in the world are successfully implementing reuse technology and are in the process of continuous improvement. However, rich nations offset the pollution-related water stress through huge investments in water technology without remedying the underlying causes, and the developing nations continue to remain vulnerable (Vorosmarty *et al.*, 2010). Therefore, it is important for Kerala to look for cost-effective technology, given its unique topographic alignment and policy to address source sustainability.

Precision Management for Traditional Natural Resources

Precision management is an emerging area in traditional natural resource management of land and water. Agriculture is one sector where precision management has brought out significant results manifested in enhanced productivity and optimum use of inputs. Irrigation water management, fertilizer use, and cropping systems are areas warranting the introduction of precision management.

Harnessing New Natural Resources

Kerala has a long coastline of 560 km. The exclusive economic zone spreads over 2.18 lakh km^2. There is a huge scope for developing the blue economy. It is not only the fisheries sector, tourism, and maritime transport but also the offshore renewable energy, aquaculture, seabed resources, marine biotechnology, and bioprocessing which require due attention.

Tapping of the wave energy deserves urgent attention. The per capita energy consumption in the State is growing at an annual rate of 4.65 per cent. It is going to increase further with socio-economic development. There is little scope to further expand the production of hydroelectricity. Ocean energy can be a viable source for future development. Experimental data have been gathered for some sites. It may be explored for other areas also. Solar power is another energy-producing sector with huge potential for the State as it enjoys long hours of sunshine. The scope of expanding wind energy also needs proper exploration. There are many such areas in other sectors of natural resources that deserve special attention.

Green Economy

Knowledge-based economy, green economy, green technology, and creation of green jobs are interrelated. The importance of a green economy is well appreciated to transition to a low-carbon economy and reduce environmental risk and ecological drawdown. The creation of green jobs is considered essential to achieve a green economy. Many countries are gradually shifting to a green economy as part of the knowledge economy. It warrants the involvement of higher education centres and sustainability-oriented research departments.

Reorientation and Building of Institutions

To accomplish all these tasks, it is necessary to set up processes that support interactions among the existing organizations, facilitate access to the existing knowledge, create new scientific knowledge, build up capabilities and new institutions for interactive learning, and disseminate and share knowledge. Assessment of the present knowledge level in the natural resource sector, identification of the gaps, and exploration of the scope and need for innovation are part of this process. There is a need to prioritize the sectors and activities to concentrate on as financial and human resources are limited. Universities, professional organizations, educational institutions, and social organizations have an important role not only in the production of knowledge and germinating technological ideas but also in providing improved access to these ideas and creating the necessary ecosystem for new innovations.

One of the strengths of Kerala is its education system. The State is blessed with a sound academic base and strong science and technology institutes administered both by the State and Central Governments. There are professional organizations dealing with every major sector of natural resources like land, water, forest, fisheries, minerals etc. University departments are imparting higher education in many of these sectors and allied disciplines. Natural resource-based industries have been set up. However, there are hardly any meaningful interactions/collaborations among these organizations. Strengthening of collaboration and sharing of useful knowledge is important. Equally important is capacity building and skill upgradation of the people. Development of specialized higher education, sustainability research centres, and exchange of knowledge among the Universities and research institutes are part of the innovation ecosystem. It is necessary to enhance the prescriptive knowledge base and harness/use new kinds of natural resources. Building up local-level organization for the creation of new scientific knowledge relevant to the problem-solving of local-level natural resource-based industries assumes great significance in this context. The State may also consider establishing a Centre for Advanced Studies to help in this process at the policy planning level.

REFERENCES

Mokyr, J. (2002). *The Gifts of Athena: The Historical Origins of the Knowledge Economy.* Princeton: Princeton University Press.

Thomas Isaac, T.M. (2021). *Budget Speech,* Government of Kerala, Thiruvananthapuram: Government Press.

Ville, S. and Wicken, O. (2015). "The Institutional Foundations of Natural Resource Based Knowledge Economies". In *Natural Resources and Economic Growth: Learning from History,* Eds: M. Badía-Miró, V. Pinilla and H. Willebald, Routledge, doi: 10.4324/9781315769356-14

Vorosmarty, C.J., McIntyre, P.B., Gessner, M.O., Dudgeon, D., Prusevich, A., Green, P., Glidden, S., Bunn, S.E., Sullivan, C.A., Liermann, C.R., & Davies, P.M. (2010). "Global Threats to Human Water Security and River Biodiversity". *Nature,* Vol. 467, Sept. 30, pp. 555-561, doi:10.1038/nature09440.

Thankom Gopinath Arun

It is good to see that Kerala state is taking many steps in developing a knowledge economy framework. It is undoubtedly a much-awaited one, and Dr. Isaac's Budget would be considered a game-changer to the States' Vision in explicit terms. The presentations are awe-inspiring, and I have learned quite a lot about innovation in the State's ecosystem. The term knowledge economy brings the images of Silicon Valley, the tall-rise buildings, and high-tech start-ups. However, these are part of a wide range of activities that foster economic growth based on the knowledge economy.

We may need to support the knowledge economy concept in a more holistic spirit, and the entire society needs to embrace the idea. The European Bank for Reconstruction and Development (EBRD) considers the increase in total factor productivity as an indicator of the knowledge economy. Most times, more than the leading innovations, what we require is technological dynamism and a broader approach to innovation. The development or adaptation of a new product, process, marketing methods, and organizational structure changes is part of a more comprehensive innovation approach. We can relate the knowledge economy idea in Kerala's context beyond a narrow and measurable path.

Paul Romer, the economist who got the Nobel Prize, published two seminal articles in the *Journal of Political Economy* in 1986 and 1990 on long-run growth and endogenous technological change. He approached the knowledge economy like the one built around ideas that do not have a diminishing return (Jones, 2019). This is a turning point from our understanding of Solow's growth model

---

Thankom Gopinath Arun, Professor, University of Essex, UK. **E-mail:** t.g.arun@essex.ac.uk

and diminishing returns to capital. Kerala is a unique case in this context. Over time, the State popularized many ideas with people's help; the most common feature of these ideas is the generation of networks.

The networks across individuals and institutions need to be further developed into sustained knowledge hubs. Our universities and research institutions have the daunting task of knowledge production. Ideally, this has two steps. The first one is to achieve the local knowledge's full potential, followed by engaging and contributing to global knowledge production. We have transformed and made some significant inroads in utilizing tacit knowledge and local ideas compared to many other regions in the World. However, considering our underutilized infrastructure of public sector enterprises, there is further scope for developing research collaborations with Universities and other institutes. Many public sector enterprises can provide domain support to begin start-ups with the University talent using their unspent resources, opening up new ideas. Our mammoth global exposure as a community would be a useful asset in linking up with global networks. Taking advantage of digital technology, we may link up more closely and regularly with the leading knowledge networks.

The fact is that markets provide less finance for innovation that would be socially desirable. The venture capitalists are not willing to invest significant amounts in start-ups in India. That is why many governments use different intervention types to increase the amount of finance available for innovation activities. Although institutions such as KIIFB can address some of these issues, it is a long way to go. Over time, Kerala built a fantastic alternative model for social and economic development, and our ideas attracted global attention. The pandemic reveals the gaps in the public health system of very advanced economies. However, the management of the pandemic and state preparedness with limited resources is an indicator of our inherent strengths and the right policies. So, I hope the same applies to the knowledge economy in the coming years. Creating an inclusive knowledge economy should not be a technical agenda, but it is more about enhancing an individual's potential or a household or a society through collective imagination.

Thank you, Professor Joseph and GIFT, for arranging this kind of session with industry, policy, and academicians.

I hope this will support the comprehensive development of an integrated environment for policies and practices in the knowledge economy.

REFERENCES

Jones, C.I. (2019). "Paul Romer: Ideas, Nonrivalry, and Endogenous Growth". *The Scandinavian Journal of Economics*, https://doi.org/10.1111/sjoe.12370

Anoop Ambika

I think the whole industry, as well as the young and the old of the State, is equally excited about the possibilities that Dr. Isaac opened up through the budget. And I think we have a lot of work in implementing it. I think there is a disconnect between the industry and the innovation ecosystem. We have tried multiple methods, and some of those methods included presenting these innovations to the corporation in the past. Kerala Start-up Mission has introduced a process wherein companies can come and present their problems to the existing innovators and see if there is an already existing solution that can be provided, but none of that seems to be working very well.

We had some reasonable success in the past, but I do not think it has worked to the extent that we needed it to work. Product sustainability or the product market fit is not often tested before developing. We need to have an early fail mechanism where the customers will validate the idea and say that it has the potential to bring in revenue to sustain in the future. One of the things we need to implement as part of the innovative ecosystem is to connect with the early adopters of the industry or whoever is going to be the users of the innovation.

Often, innovation is misunderstood as IT software or digital technologies. We need to have a serious campaign, saying that the Kerala Start-up Mission is not just a technology mission. It is beyond that. You can go into manufacturing, solid waste management, or any kind of innovation that happens across multiple processes. There needs to be a campaign that happens either from K-DISC or from Start-up Mission, which will empower people to try out things beyond technology.

Anoop Ambika, Chief Executive Officer, Clap Research and Genpro Research, Kerala.
E-mail: anoop.ambika@clapresearch.com

IIT Hyderabad recently came up with a model wherein they will provide a professor, along with three or four students, as part of a course curriculum wherein they can engage with a startup. The start-up can tell you the problems, and they will build the prototype for you. There are various sensitive issues, like IPR, involved in this, but that could possibly be one of the easy ways of getting a product prototype without spending too much money. If our higher education institutions like KTU can come up with such a plan, it is going to be an easy method by which we will be able to prototype some of the products.

A group of entrepreneurs said that they had a product and got orders and something to do with the testing of the machine. But, they had no clue that they had to apply for start-up India, and they had to get a unique ID in order to get access to capital. I suggest that the start-up mission come up with a handbook that can be an electronic booklet so that people can later modify and circulate it to entrepreneurs.

Mentorship is another area. We have had a very poor experience in finding mentors and holding the companies. We should also seriously consider providing equity for these mentors. Based on a discussion between the start-up founders and the mentor, they see the value of this mentor being involved in the start-up company. I think we should have a formalized mechanism by which we will be able to give equity to these mentors.

We have to identify some of the sectors where we had huge success and then put more trust in those sectors, and this is where the cluster concept will come into the picture. A lot of companies have already started their innovation centres in Bengaluru. We should have a mechanism by which we should be able to engage with these innovation centres of large companies and expose our innovations to those on a routine basis.

IQ has tremendously multiplied over the years, and some of the future innovations could even come from the 10th or 12th-standard students. We need to have an ongoing mechanism by which we will engage with centres like Atal Tinkering Labs, which will be established in schools, pick up innovations from them, and create an innovative or entrepreneurial ecosystem within schools. We are putting a lot of spotlight on Artificial Intelligence, Machine Learning, and analytics. We need to start seriously thinking about collecting data. We have a lot of data; we have data coming in from satellites, data being collected about our livestock, our flora, fauna, and all that stuff. Unless we have this data curated, collected, and stored in a data hub, nobody will be able to develop what is called an Artificial Intelligence model. We need to have this data collected and stored in a cloud platform that can be controlled by the government and open to everyone so that people can come in and do innovations on top of that data. A data hub is something that the government and industry can join together and create, which can be used by everybody to create AI and ML models.

Rainer Walz

Introduction

The knowledge economy has become a widespread topic for countries from the North. However, it is also relevant for countries of the South, and the case of Kerala and the focus on the knowledge economy in its most recent budget speech (Isaac Thomas, 2021) is a remarkable document that countries of the South are taking up the challenges involved.

Very often, the knowledge economy is linked to digital technologies. Sometimes, the term digital transformation is used. This shows that we have to consider the changes in a broad perspective, which accounts for the co-evolution of technologies, institutions, the economy, and societies on a much wider scale. In this contribution, the focus will be on what all of this means for policy-making, in particular on the need to combine key enabling digital competencies with other crosscutting innovations and traditional sector strengths.

Key Challenges for Successful Policy Strategies

Within the many requirements to be addressed, there are three areas that are highly important for such successful transformations but which are often neglected in national or regional policymaking:

Rainer Walz, Deputy Director, Fraunhofer Institute for Systems and Innovation Research, Germany. **E-mail:** Rainer.Walz@isi.fraunhofer.de

- Embedding domestic policies within the requirement of transformations shaped by international megatrends;
- Balancing supply-side innovation policies with demand-side innovation policies; and
- Integrating innovation policies with sector-specific industrial policies.

If we consider the perspectives of basing Kerala on a knowledge economy, we have to look at the international megatrends shaping transformations. First, there are not only technical but also social innovations taking place. Indeed, the importance of social innovations in tackling future challenges seems to be emphasized, and the Corona pandemic shows the importance of changing behaviour (Bodenheimer & Leidenberger, 2020). Second, increasing South-South trade points towards a new pattern of trade emerging. At the same time, the future of trade regimes has become more uncertain, which is also reflected in the debate about technology sovereignty, which has been emerging recently (Edler *et al.*, 2020). Third, in a lot of countries, we see that digital competencies are seen as a key enabling competency that has to be combined with very specific competencies within each country. Fourth, we also see a renewed urge to mobilize innovation policy not only for economic well-being but to pursue well-defined societal goals. The newly debated paradigm of mission-oriented innovation policies links innovation strongly to global challenges. In line with the first megatrend, this also explains why social innovations are increasingly debated within the sustainability discourse. Indeed, the debate about post-growth societies (see, e.g. Crownshaw *et al.*, 2019) points towards the challenge of how to make an increase in quality of life more independent from an increase in GDP.

At first glance, taking up all these megatrends might look to be far detached from specific programmes of Kerala. However, it is exactly the programme level that decides whether or not strategic policy goals are implemented in policies. Thus, we have to translate these strategic imperatives into all of the programmes that Kerala uses to move forward, such as the young innovator programmes and start-up mission programmes. These programmes have to reflect on how they position themselves within these megatrends. Aligning with the megatrends is a prerequisite for strategic prioritization in the implementation of the programmes.

The second major issue is that it is not enough to look at the supply side of new innovations only. With regard to the application of the competencies that are built up in the programmes, it is very important to have an early demand for these applications. Supporting early learning in the market and mobilizing user-producer interaction is thus a key dimension for any innovation policy. This requires balancing supply-side innovation policies with demand-side innovation policies (Edler & Georghiou, 2007). One key instrument is public procurement. To refer to the start-up programme of Kerala, Start-ups need a perspective that there will be demand for their products. From a systemic perspective, learning in the market is a key prerequisite, and public procurement can contribute to producer-user interaction, which will improve innovation continually. Finally, guidance of search has been identified as an important function to be fulfilled by a successful innovation system. Public procurement, which specifies the characteristics of products or services in advance, is highly important with regard to guidance in the search for new solutions. In particular, in countries with fewer lead users with high income, the State and public procurement have to substitute for the function of private lead users even more. Clearly, this task goes beyond the task of a single programme. There is a need for an integrated policy of the State of Kerala to think about a whole set of products with challenging new specifications, for which Kerala would be willing to promise public demand if the innovators are able to come up with new solutions that fulfil these specifications.

The third major issue deals with the sectors to be addressed by policy. This topic is also related to the integration of innovation and industrial policy. Applications of the innovations involve different sectors and segments of the economy. Innovations are needed in both new and established sectors and industries. A knowledge economy is not only about the high-tech industry. It is the combination of ideas originating in high-tech industries with competencies in sectors that are traditionally strong that make an economy successful. In Germany, for example, the machinery industry is a core area of competency. Thus, a lot of the emphasis put on digitization is its application in the machinery industry, and the slogan of Industry 4.0 is a very important aspect in Germany because it reflects the specific combination of the sectoral and key enabling competencies. The experience with a mission-oriented innovation policy indicates that this poses a big challenge for governance. With regard to policymaking, policies that support innovations have to be integrated with policies for specific sectors. Take the case of Kerala: It is not only the programme owners of young innovation programmes and start-up mission programmes that have to do their job. There is a need to integrate the policies of different ministries. Steering such an integration requires strategic intelligence, as well as institutions coordinating different ministries. Finding the successful combinations of existing competencies in traditional sectors, new competencies to be developed in innovation programmes, and strategic positioning within the megatrends becomes a key challenge for transforming Kerala into a knowledge-based economy.

Two Case Examples: Garment Industry and Green Innovations

The 2020-21 Budget speech of Kerala referred to the importance of the textile industries, among others. The textile and garment industry is a very good example of how these general strategic rationales relate to specific sectors. On a worldwide scale, we see the megatrend that the demand for textiles is becoming more diverse. In addition to calls for fair trade along the value chain, there are problems with harmful chemicals in textiles—from the use of pesticides in growing raw materials up to the use to change fabric characteristics (Roos *et al.*, 2020). Globally, we see a segment of market demand emerging, which is putting an increased emphasis on fair working conditions along the supply chain of textiles and environmentally sound textiles. This might open up new perspectives for the textile and garment industry in countries of the South, which are willing to strive to improve environmental and working conditions in their home country. On the other hand, we see that new challenges arise for these very traditional industries in order to move in this direction. Digital solutions are needed (Larson, 2018), such as blockchain technology, which enables certification of improved environmental or working conditions along the value chain. Clearly, a higher share of value-added can be captured by the economies that move first in that direction.

So, what does this mean with regard to the situation of Kerala? On the one hand, Kerala needs competencies in digital technologies, young innovators, and start-up innovators who come up with new ideas, e.g. for using blockchain technology. But, it has to be done in combination with traditional players, for example, from the textile industry. Furthermore, it also requires that the digital knowledge is diffusing across all segments of a population that are involved in the industry. So, improving digital knowledge across all populations, among the labour force, which is a key goal of Kerala moving towards a knowledge economy, is not only necessary for equity reasons. It is also a prerequisite for the success of sectorial innovation strategies in specific industries. Identifying such bundles of complementarities and giving them high priority within the budget and overall policies will be key to the success of Kerala's strategy.

The second megatrend mentioned above is that South-South trade is increasing. That also holds for green technologies and green solutions. Green innovations are increasingly coming from countries of the South (Walz *et al.*, 2017). Recent research indicates that the role of frugal innovations in green innovations is increasing (Gandenberger *et al.*, 2020), and India as a country has a very important history and very high competencies in developing frugal innovation. These frugal innovations might not amount to a huge part of all innovations in each sector. But they can occur in each sector, and their sum might be significant for a state. Sometimes, it is argued that these frugal innovations are very low-tech and not knowledge-intensive at all. But frugal innovations are environmentally friendly and, at the same time, also knowledge-intensive. It might not be knowledge that is codified in patents. Very often, frugals are characterized by linking technical and social innovations. Thus, if one looks at the technical side only, this propels you to judge them as not so knowledge-intensive. However, it is the combination of both technical and social innovations that creates new knowledge, and this is exactly in line with the first megatrend mentioned above, the linking of technical and social innovations. To take advantage of this strategic approach, it would be a good opportunity to strengthen the role of such frugal innovations within Kerala's innovation programmes, but also within the different sectorial programmes. This is another example of combining the strengths of Kerala with global trends and with the build-up of a knowledge economy where future success can be found. And it is, again, early government procurement that has to be part of such a programme package. Building a combination of programmes that make Kerala into something like a hub of sustainable, frugal innovations—would that not be a vision to go for?

Integrating Knowledge-based Economy and Sustainable Development into the Kerala Model for Development

The need for innovations to achieve the Sustainable Development Goals has been mentioned above. Given the magnitude of challenges, this goes beyond single innovations. We need transformations in the way we build our economies. Indeed, increasingly, it is argued that new paradigms for the development of economies are needed. Albeit taking place in small circles so far only, post-growth paradigms are debated (Zitat). It is no longer the case that there is a consensus that a higher GDP also means higher well-being. Instead of looking at higher growth rates alone, development paths that achieve SDG are getting the focus. Given the importance of innovations for the SDG, we have to look at future development from another perspective: What is the possibility of having high levels of innovations, with perhaps not-so-high economic growth?

The Kerala model of development has won praise internationally as a role model for achieving a high human development index (HDI). The HDI measures human well-being, taking into account economics, education, and health as broad dimensions. In addition, it takes the distribution within each of these categories into account and builds an inequality-adjusted index. Indeed, data shows that Kerala was leading all Indian states with an HDI of 0.782, well above the national Indian index value of 0.646 (Global DataLab, 2021). Most important, however, is that Kerala achieved this with lower economic growth rates. Indeed, the stream of literature over the years indicates that—despite all remaining challenges—the core of Kerala's success in its development model can be found in its emphasis on public policies fostering sectors such as health and education (Payaril, 1996; Ramachandran, 1998; Veron, 2001; Sen, 2006; Thresia, 2018; Chathukulam & Tharamangalam, 2021). Could Kerala also be a role model for achieving a high level of innovation in a post-growth world?

The knowledge economy is associated with many innovations. What does the goal of transforming Kerala into a knowledge economy mean to the "Kerala model" of development? This article pointed out the need to combine key enabling digital competencies with innovations and traditional sector strengths. The same holds for the "Kerala model" of development. If Kerala is able to enhance its successful development model now with the competencies of a knowledge economy, it might come up with the "Kerala model of development 2.0". Thus, Kerala might become a very important role model for achieving SDGs. Surely, this requires a lot of work to be done and does not come easily. But thinking about this perspective underlines that the mission to base Kerala on a knowledge-based economy involves much more than a regional strategy only.

REFERENCES

Bodenheimer, M.; Leidenberger, J. (2020): "COVID-19 as a Window of Opportunity for Sustainability Transitions? Narratives and Communication Strategies beyond the Pandemic". *Sustainability, 16*(1), 61-66.

Chathukulam, J. and Tharamangalam, J. (2021): "The Kerala Model in the Time of COVID-19: Rethinking State, Society and Democracy". *World Development, 137*, 105-207

Crownshaw, T. *et al.* (2019). "Over the Horizon: Exploring the Conditions of a Post-growth World". *The Anthropocene Review, 6*(1-2), 117-41.

Edler, J. *et al.* (2020). Technology Sovereignty: From Demand to Concept. Perspectives—Policy Brief, No. 02/2020. https://www.isi.fraunhofer.de/content/dam/isi/dokumente/publikationen/technology_sovereignty.pdf

Edler, J.; Georghiou, G. (2007). "Public Procurement and Innovation—Resurrecting the Demand Side". *Research Policy, 36* (7), 949-63.

Gandenberger, C., Kroll, H. and Walz, R. (2020). "The Role of Frugal Innovation in the Global Diffusion of Green Technologies", *Int. J. Technology Management, 83*(1/2/3) 97-113.

Global Data Lab (2021). Subnational HDI (2019). Data retrieved on July 19, 2021 from https://globaldatalab.org/shdi/shdi/?levels=1%2B4&interpolation=1&extrapolation=0&nearest_real=0

Isaac Thomas, T.M. (2021). *Budget Speech 2021-22* of Finance Minister of Kerala, January 15, 2021, Government of Kerala.

Larson, J.K.L. (2018). "Digital Innovation for Sustainable Apparel Systems. Experiences based on Projects in Textile Value Chain Development". *Research Journal of Textile and Apparel, 22*(4), 370-89.

Payaril, G. (1996). "The 'Kerala model' of Development: Development and Sustainability in the Third World". *Third World Quarterly, 17*(5), pp. 941-58, doi: 10.1080/01436599615191

Ramachandran, V.K. (1998). "On Kerala's Development Achievements". In J. Dreze & A. Sen (Eds.), *Indian Development: Selected Regional Perspective*, pp. 205-356, Delhi: Oxford University Press.

Roos, S. *et al.* (2020). "A Function-Based Approach for Life Cycle. Management of Chemicals in the Textile Industry". *Sustainability, 12*, 1273.

Sen, A. (2006). "Education in Kerala's Development: Towards a New Agenda". In: Tharamangalam (Ed.). *Kerala: The Paradoxes in Public Action and Development,* pp. 258-72. New Delhi: Orient Longman.

Thresia, C. (2018). "Health Inequalities in South Asia at the Launch of Sustainable Development Goals: Exclusions in Health in Kerala, India Need Political Interventions". *International Journal of Health Services, 48*(1), 57-80.

Veron, R. (2001). "The New Kerala Model: Lessons for Sustainable Development". *World Development, 29*(4), 601-17.

Walz, R.; Pfaff, M.; Marscheider-Weidemann, F.; Glöser-Chahoud, S. (2017): Innovations for Reaching the Green Sustainable Development Goals—Where Will They Come From? *International Economics and Economic Policy, 14*(3), 684-95.

Rasmus Lema

The sections of the Kerala Budget 2021-22 that pertain to 'Transforming Kerala into a Knowledge Economy' contain a vision of a knowledge economy that is both ambitious and laudable. This vision is unfolded in the Budget Speech by Prof. Finance Minister Issac, and among various important elements, higher education and innovation feature prominently. My intervention will be brief and focus on this element: transforming higher education for the knowledge economy. As such, my intervention connects to those speakers who have emphasized the importance of transforming the innovation system, but I will deal with higher education as one key element of this system.

I saw this consultation as an opportunity to read through the budget speech and come up with some quick thoughts and comments on this. Importantly, when I hear the notion of the knowledge economy, the question for me immediately is: knowledge for what and knowledge for whom? Certain types of knowledge are more important than others, and certain types of knowledge are more strategic than others in any given context and point in time.

From my perspective, starting from the societal challenges that Kerala is facing are critical. Both economic, social, and environmental challenges. Thinking through these challenges and their implications for the types of change that are needed can help us determine the kinds of knowledge that the Keralian knowledge economy should produce and diffuse and the role that

---

Rasmus Lema, Department of Business and Management, Aalborg University, Denmark.
E-mail: lema@business.aau.dk

higher education can play in doing so. The strategy for the Keralian knowledge economy needs a clear identification of needs. The first step is mapping the challenges and prioritization of them. The next step is thinking about the implications for innovations. New ideas about innovation policy in the European Commission and elsewhere—or rather ideas that have recently resurfaced—concentrate on mission-driven innovation and selections of missions connected to societal challenges. Higher education can be a key factor in realizing such a mission.

I thought it was very interesting that in the Budget Speech, there was considerable attention paid to the need for transforming higher education in line with Kerala's recent achievements in school education. The Speech emphasized that to make progress towards the knowledge economy, higher education is key:

Investment many times higher than the present one is inevitable in higher education. Similarly, the approach to teaching research needs a paradigm shift. Both are not easy. We ought to move towards this goal with resolve. Otherwise, the developmental strategy presented in this budget will remain a mirage (Isaac, 2021, p. 24).

I agree with this, and I think it is very important. Undoubtedly, transformation to a knowledge economy requires a lot of investment—huge investments—in higher education. Investment in higher education will increase, as is clear from the budget. However, how teaching and research will shift to a new paradigm and what the paradigm is less clear. Naturally, this is also something that is beyond the remits of the Ministry of Finance, but I think we should appreciate that it is highlighted in the speech.

I would like to propose the heading of a challenge-driven higher education system that plays an active part in mission innovation. It should include both teaching and research. It is about making closer connections to other stakeholders in key challenge-driven missions. When reading through the budget speech, a very good example of what such challenge-driven learning can achieve is the example of the Bandicoot robot. It was also mentioned earlier in one of the presentations: From the starting point of a key challenge, which has to do with the sewage system in Kerala, a group of engineering students sat together to try to deal with the problem and invented this robot. They worked together with users, private sector stakeholders, and others to produce this invention. This is exactly the type of challenge-driven innovation I have in mind. It can be used for all sort of problems and include many different types of teaching and research.

What does it require for the higher education system to think in these terms to reorient the entire curriculum towards such societal challenges? Now, of course, we cannot completely move away from the existing curriculum elements. They have to be in place. But nevertheless, the ties with the users of university graduates—in public, private, and social sectors—are very important. The ties should be built into teaching. University students working together on real-life problems are very important. And they should be students working from different disciplines. Engineers working with social science students and so on. So, the transformation of the curriculum is important, including how students can work together across different disciplines and how they can connect much closer to the needs of the 'burning platforms' of the private and public sectors. So, the key elements are: (a) forging closer ties with 'users' of university graduates in private, public, and social sectors and (b) transforming curricula, including interdisciplinarity and project work. These could be fundamentals of a new paradigm in university teaching.

Innovation efforts should not only seek to address local challenges but also to bring these innovations to markets with similar challenges. Research and teaching could connect closely to both local problem-solving and national and global commercialization of innovations. This is about how to enable the business side of local problem-solving.

I am thinking about this connection with some work I have been doing together with Xiaolan Fu, who was speaking just a few minutes ago. We were looking at 'green windows of opportunity' in China: how Chinese enterprises were able to benefit economically from addressing local and global sustainability challenges. The government and other stakeholders implemented institutional and technological to address sustainability, local pollution challenges, energy security etc. Starting with local mission-driven innovation, the next step was the export of these green technologies to the rest of the World. Universities should be engaged in both steps, working with the key stakeholders. They can play key roles in a challenge-led window of opportunity creation strategy for economic and social development.

In sum, I applaud the ideas in the budget and suggest that we think about how we can situate transformation in higher education to match with a strategy where key challenges and mission-driven innovation programmes guide the transformation to a knowledge-based economy.

Nanditha Mathew

In my presentation, I hope to show how Kerala can climb the ladder to a knowledge economy. The economic growth and development of a country do not happen in one day. It involves different steps. One could think of a ladder, where at each step, individuals and, indeed, the country itself learn and accumulate knowledge while moving towards a knowledge economy. And likely, you cannot jump to the final step directly from the first. Here, I will talk about the capability approach to development from a micro or firm-level perspective. Indeed, when we talk about production, firms are the actual actors behind the production, and they play a crucial role in the accumulation of knowledge at a macro level.

It is intuitive to think that business firms know how to build things: they let us fly from one continent to the other, build computer networks to communicate from different parts of the World, and have a central role in the mass production of vaccines to fight a pandemic. Let's take the example of the firm Luxor. Luxor produces pens now. If it were to enter a new market, it could produce sophisticated calligraphy pens for drawing, and likely, it cannot produce trucks. Instead, BMW India, which produces cars, could use their capabilities to produce trucks as well. So, it is very important to understand the "already existing capabilities" to understand where one stands in terms of firms and individuals, to see where one can go next, which is the step that Kerala can take next, given where she is now.

Nanditha Mathew, United Nations University—MERIT, Netherlands.
E-mail: n.mathew@maastrichtuniversity.nl

Capabilities and skills are difficult to measure. Even though we do not observe capabilities, we know which firms produce which products. From this information, we can try to derive the capability structure of firms. Such a data-driven approach helps in measuring relatedness between products and the overall coherence of the production of the firm, i.e. how related are the products they produce. Here, the relatedness (or proximity) of products depicts the proximity of capabilities (or ability to produce products). For more details on this measure, please refer to Dosi, Mathew & Pugliese (2020). We find that firms producing a coherent set of products perform better because when they expanded their production, they moved to products that were similar in terms of capabilities to the ones they were already producing. This is why it is important to understand the existing capabilities of firms in Kerala to understand where Kerala stands to look into which are the next steps in the capability ladder she can move to.

On one side, there are firms that provide jobs, and on the other side, we have a lot of educated unemployed. Clearly, there is a lot of discrepancy between these two, or in other words, a matching issue between the jobs that are created and the skills that people have. The problem of educated unemployment is one of the biggest challenges in Kerala. The question is, which kind of policies can absorb all these educated unemployed people? When we look at the opportunity space in front of us, we should not only look at firms but also what people in Kerala can do. I believe that the Government of Kerala is on the right path with the idea put forth in the budget on providing the right skills to the people. However, one should be very careful in understanding which are the right skills. The skills should not only relate to the individual abilities of the people but also relate to what organizations or firms want, relating to what firms and organizations do now and what they can do in the future.

In the same way, we measure the capabilities of firms, this can be done at the individual level, given the abilities of an individual, which are the skills that will help her to, let's say, climb the next step of the ladder. To repeat, it is important to understand which step of the ladder you are in because only then can you evaluate which is the next level you can achieve. This is true for both firms and also for individuals.

No doubt, there are several challenges ahead. But what one could hope to build is an ecosystem that will foster innovation and growth. As Marianna Mazzucato argues, states should create markets rather than fix them, and when the State wants to create markets, it will be able to when it has the ecosystem that surrounds it.

I want to conclude by emphasizing this point—at a policy level, it is important to create all the building blocks necessary. What is required is to prepare fertile soil to be able to grow a seed when a chance arises because "chance favours the prepared mind" (Louis Pasteur). What one expects from Kerala is to lead and show the way forward so that this model can be used also for other states and for countries around the World.

C. Skilling, Reskilling and Upskilling

Revamping Higher Education Sector for a Knowledge Economy

Saji Gopinath

It is an honour to be among this eminent panel on this International Consultation on Transforming Kerala into a Knowledge Economy. We had two very excellent discussions, which were looking at two key aspects of a knowledge economy: the infrastructure aspect and, later on, the innovation ecosystem aspect. Now, I think the third and perhaps one of the most important aspects is what we will be discussing in this session—about people. In the budget, the honourable Finance Minister has basically looked at three key aspects of how we actually develop the people to drive the knowledge economy. This includes a focus on the creation of knowledge and on the knowledge workers. In this context, I think one of the key elements of our strategy proposed in the budget is to strengthen higher education institutions by creating research centres of excellence and augmenting the infrastructure in higher education institutions. In the morning, Prof. Lundvall presented how China has actually made a very successful model in the knowledge economy. I think our model is also very similar to that, where we are looking at enhancing public investment in the higher education sector.

We are also looking at setting up a large number of post-doctoral fellowships in the areas which are going to be very relevant in the context of the current Kerala development puzzle. Now, in all these discussions today, I think one

The author is the Vice Chancellor of Kerala University of Digital Science, Innovation and Technology. **E-mail:** saji.gopinath@iiitmk.ac.in

key element that has come out is that for any development to be inclusive, the knowledge economy or knowledge society has to be extremely inclusive. Perhaps that was one of the reasons why there is a focus on setting up key centres of excellence in areas that are going to take Kerala forward. The centres are expected to be in areas that are going to affect multiple sectors of Kerala. Be it the areas of disaster resilience or marine development or supporting the traditional art forms, how do you actually look at doing high-end research to enable high-end knowledge creation so that these sectors can actually move up in the value chain? This, I think, is the second key proposed in the budget. Unfortunately, we may not be discussing these two aspects in this session; perhaps the last session will discuss these in more detail.

The third element of knowledge society proposed, I think, may perhaps solve a paradox that Kerala has been facing all these years. So, the creation of a large number of knowledge workers or knowledge resources is actually going to be the key challenge when we want to create this knowledge economy. We know that the higher amount of state investment in education will create more knowledge workers. We already have a very high level of secondary education; even in higher education, GER (Gross Enrollment Ratio) of around 37 per cent is much more than the national average. Attempts are being made to raise it to 75 per cent, which means three out of four people in Kerala will actually have access to higher education. While this enhances the numbers, we are also concerned that we have a high unemployment rate and a lack of participation of educated youth, especially women, in economic activities. This is basically one of the key areas this session is going to address.

The knowledge economy is basically different from an industrial economy, which all of us know pretty well. We know that from large industrial centres, which basically concentrate work in a few places, there is a transition happening in the workplace with the work getting distributed all around through new work from homes and work near homes modes. Distributed employment centres are actually getting created in many places, provided you have people with the right skills in those places to take the type of work that is available across the globe. I believe that this is an area where Kerala should actually focus in a serious manner. The Budget has put some very ambitious targets to do that.

We have a large number of educated youth, but they may have to be skilled. I think Dr. Nandita rightly pointed out in her observation in the last session they have to be skilled in the right things, and there should be continuous feedback among the industry, the workgivers, and work-demanding units, in a continuous manner. This is another aspect this session is going to discuss.

Based on this broad theme, we have two presentations. One which looks at what would be the type of skilling strategy for the State and, going forward, how we actually ensure that we will make the correct number of knowledge workers and exploit these opportunities that are emerging from different parts of the globe. The second part is how we create decentralized workspaces so that the people can actually remain in the State, even though they may be delivering their work output elsewhere. They can contribute to knowledge creation; they can actually look at the jobs around them. At the same time, they could also look at their participation in the global economy without even moving out of the State. So, these two things are basically getting presented now. And then, we will get into the comments from the various members of the expert panel from different parts of the world. So, let me first invite Sri Santosh Kurup, the CEO of the ICT Academy of Kerala. ICT academy is a public-private partnership that looks at skilling on various levels of the knowledge economy. So, over to you, Mr. Santhosh.

Kerala Workforce Strategies for the Fourth Industrial Revolution

Santhosh Chandrasekhara Kurup

I picked up three critical trends in the new workforce evolution. I wanted to talk about the progress of the Internet, mobile, and social media, especially in country number 2, compared to the rest of the world. We are sitting in a state with the maximum density of mobile penetration in the whole country. So, this is one interesting trend that has revolutionized the digitization process, new business models, and the world's transformation into the new internet economy. The second part is the impact of Industry 4.0, which is sometimes misunderstood or misconstrued as an IT revolution. But this is not the case; this industrial revolution is happening quickly. I think we have seen three industrial revolutions, and this one is about converging the physical world to the cyber world and the biological world. Primarily because the cyber world has grown so much, and on average, there is a statistic which states that people spend around six and half hours on mobile these days.

The World Economic Forum 2020 report says that around 85 million jobs would perhaps get displaced or shifted. But the beauty is that about 97 million new roles would emerge as part of the industry 4.0. So, what I mean to construct is the fact that there is a massive change in dynamics in terms of the roles and

---

Mr. Santhosh Chandrasekara Kurup is the Chief Executive Officer, ICT Academy of Kerala.
E-mail: santhosh chandrasekhara kuruph@gmail.com

responsibilities and the work that is going on in the Industrial Revolution 4.0. The second construct is not about information technology-related jobs. This is about IR 4.0 interfering and intervening successfully in multiple sectors, from agri-business to mining to petroleum and natural gas businesses. So, this is going to spread across various domains, and that is the reason why new jobs are getting created in different sectors, not just IT.

The third one is about digital acceleration and innovation, primarily driven by the pandemic. One of the interesting trends that has come in as part of it is the acceleration of digitization that has happened. But thanks to COVID-19, it became the biggest transformation agent in bringing a lot of acceleration in the digital space.

So, physical world interactions have become digitized, and we are connecting more virtually. Companies like Zoom, for example, have grown 35 times during this time. So, there are a lot of changes that have happened in the digitization process. Telemedicine, for example, is another interesting case that grew by 400 per cent, as per one of the reports.

It also created a new set of innovations into it. Frugal innovation became a little more accelerated during this period. In Kerala, we had a very interesting trend whereby start-up mission-sponsored companies came together and created ventilators that were produced at very affordable prices. They used technologies like 3D printing and IoT to create such mechanisms fairly quickly. So, frugal innovation is another area that is picked up as part of this strength. Lastly, the changing workforce dynamics, such as working from home and remote working, became the new normal. Approximately 84 per cent of employers are set to rapidly digitize their workforce so that the work can be pushed remotely. Even after the pandemic sets in and goes out, it is likely that this trend will continue, and approximately 44 per cent of the workforce will remotely operate permanently.

The next context is higher education. Even though we call it a higher education paradox, as the famous scientist says, in the midst of every crisis lies great opportunity; so we feel that this issue of having low participation, especially women's participation in the economic activity. Secondly, in terms of skill development, Kerala has been at the forefront in many areas when it comes to various indices that we talked about. Kerala started these skills development activities long ago before a lot of other states picked up. We have a number of initiatives focusing on sector-wise skilling and development activity. Approximately a hundred thousand participants go through the skilling programme every year from Kerala. An interesting fact is that 23,000 new self-employed enterprises were generated during the COVID-19 pandemic. 2500 plus active start-ups work in the State and are considered to be one of the top performers in the country.

Another important issue is the return of Keralites with international exposure. Nearly 6,00,000 people came back and had to stay back due to the pandemic, but these are people who have not just skills but an understanding of the international work culture. This is what is going to create a new set of job roles and a new set of job opportunities. The second one is about the gig economy push, even in India. This is picking up fairly big; in fact, 50 million Indians already work on gigs in India. We are in the seventh position, and there is a lot more potential for us to look at this.

So, knowledge enablement, right from literacy to research, is a set of enablement that the State is undertaking that is leading to an outcome of jobs of various types. From an industry perspective, it is also important for the State to look at what the industry needs, especially in the new technology area and talent ecosystem. Government support and benefits are some of the areas that the government is looking into. There are three broad contours workflow strategies that the Kerala government is pushing forward, and it was alluded to by the Finance Minister.

When we were looking at employment targets, we looked at only permanent jobs, but now the strategy is not just looking at the permanent jobs alone but looking at work and effort-based career types as well. The second dimension is that when we look at employment again, we look at creating employment in the offices within Kerala. Now, remote working has enabled people to work from anywhere. So we are not looking at just the statewide employment opportunity, but going global and looking at the global opportunities and how to enable our youth for the same. The third dimension is that the career is not just about information technology on IR4.

We are talking about 60 to 65 million jobs being created in 2025. Of these, around 25 to 28 million jobs are going to be newly created with these three dimensions within India. Kerala is super poised towards achieving that target. One of the key enablers is obviously the infrastructure backbone. Some of the IT infrastructure backbone, which is required for remote working and distributed workforce management, is also provisioned. Government-supported skills training is also another important element of our strategy. But in this strategy, the fundamental differences are that we are actually onboarding the work types ahead of time and then working reversely to skill our candidates by matching them to the work types. So, it is much more collaborative and synchronized compared to the skilling programmes that we have seen in the past. There is going to be a huge IT push connecting both the work seekers and the providers. I believe a lot of legal frameworks have been developed for new work-type activities across the world. But providing social security and other government benefits is something that is going to be unique for the whole strategy that the State is trying to build up, and that is the core of the strategy. There are a lot of operational layers that we are working on, and there is a huge set of targets that we are aiming at.

Work-near-home Infrastructure for Kerala

P.M. Sasi

I will start by working from home. It has been there for quite some time, but the difference is that the work-from-home facility was offered by very few companies and was offered to very few people. Techno Park had a plan for constructing a building, and we had surveyed the demand for space. We had a lot of discussions with many industry leaders, who stated that working from home will become popular in the coming years, which has to be taken into account. COVID-19 made these changes happen all of a sudden. We postponed our decision to have our own building.

Most of the IT companies in Kerala are working from the IT parks set up by the government. There are three major IT parks- Techno Park, Info Park, and Cyber Park, accommodating about 900 companies employing more than 110,000 employees. Due to the pandemic, most people are now working from home, and only 5 to 10 per cent are working from the offices. We were expecting that by early 2021, most of the people would be back in office. However, the pandemic threat still exists, and IT companies have postponed their decision to work from an office.

The productivity of working from home has been reported to be very good by almost all the companies. Apart from productivity, some of the companies are

---

Mr. P.M Sasi is the CEO of IT Parks and Director, International Centre for Free and Open Source Software (ICFOSS), Kerala. **E-mail:** sasipm@cdac.in

also saving many of the other expenses like transportation costs, administrative costs etc. And some other companies have scaled down their rented office spaces as they are not using the complete space now.

But there are certain concerns also starting from the issue of infrastructure at homes to the connectivity issues, issues of working overtime, issues resulting in the socialization of people etc. One of the main concerns that has been raised by the companies is in developing the organizational culture and the organizational values. Normally, these are developed when people come to the office, they interact with others, they collaborate with each other, they create a bond, they also learn from the seniors, and so on. But in the virtual environment, when you are working from home, these do not happen, and it is very difficult to imbibe the culture and values among the employees.

Dr. Santosh said that 44 per cent will be working from home even after COVID-19 is controlled. However, there are various research/studies conducted on this, and the general consensus is that between 70 to 90 per cent of the people will be coming to the office once the situation is under control, and the remaining people will be working from home. Demand for huge campuses may not be there in the short-term, especially in the case of IT.

But then it is going to be the hybrid mode of working in the future. As we discussed, some of the employees will be working from home or other places, and some of the employees will be working from their offices. This may be on a rotation basis also.

The industries are now hesitant to commit to long-term investments. They are looking for minimal commitments in the short-term till the COVID scare is over. They are also looking for space on demand so that they can upscale/downscale the space availability as per the requirement. This will be of immense help to the industry as they have to pay only for their usage.

This is the same situation where we migrated from our own/dedicated infrastructure to the cloud infrastructure. For the dedicated infrastructure, we had to pay the cost upfront for the whole infrastructure. Even if you are using the infrastructure for possibly a day or an hour, you need to pay for the whole infrastructure, and the infrastructure will be with you whether you are using it or not.

The cloud facility offered the flexibility for the user community to procure resources as per demand without any upfront commitment and the flexibility of paying as per usage. I think this is coming in the physical infrastructure space also these days. Now, the industry is looking for flexibility of usage, such that space may be utilized by any of their employees as per the requirement. They also want to use the facility temporarily or for a longer period as the demand rises. They also will need the facilities like conference rooms, training facility other services on demand.

The new-age employees are looking for facilities where they can walk to work so that they are not far away from the comfort of their homes, and they also do not have to worry about issues of commuting to their workplaces. They are also looking for proximity to all the amenities so that they can walk to buy and the time for commuting can be saved.

The traditional jobs have been regular, full-time, or part-time. But in the gig economy, people can take a variety of short-term jobs and projects. Indian freelancer market is expected to grow to US dollars 20 to $30 billion by 2025. Working from home may not be suitable for many because of the issues that I said earlier.

Interestingly, companies are turning to tier two and tier three cities for their expansion, which was never the case before. Earlier, many of the companies were looking for places like Bangaluru and Hyderabad, and the tier two and tier three cities were not in their plan, which has changed now. It is also understood that the majority of the freelancers in India are from tier two and tier three cities.

In the Kerala context, there is abundant talent available. Because of the reverse migration from many foreign countries, mainly from the Middle East countries, there has been a jump in skilled and highly skilled human resources. There is a big push for a digital economy, as we have seen in the recent budget. A skill mission is planned to meet the requirements of the knowledge economy.

The work-near-home facility is a proposal for interconnected centres distributed across Kerala. All centres are connected to the cloud, and we will offer flexible workspaces to organizations as well as individuals. Definitely, this will strengthen the freelance ecosystem in Kerala because the freelancers may not be comfortable working from home for various reasons, as explained above. If they get a space where they can work with sufficient security, sufficient safety, and a high level of connectivity, this could definitely be the place where freelance workers can operate.

This will attract employment to Kerala, as employees can work from anywhere in the new mode of working. So, a Keralite staying in Kerala can get work anywhere in the world yet still work from Kerala. With the support of proper infrastructure, Kerala can be a centre for freelancers working for organizations anywhere in the world. For organizations, this gives them the option to scout for the best talent, and they can optimize the cost of human resources.

The facilities proposed to be available in these centres may be available from other co-working centres also. But what makes it unique to the Work Near Home concept in Kerala is the service support that will be offered to the users, especially the freelancers and start-ups. They will need a lot of support in legal assistance, taxation and filing, company registration, and consulting, among others. These services will be offered to the users as a central facility.

We plan the WNH centres to be small modules so that occupancy and return on investment can be ensured in minimal time. We have identified that 5,000 square feet is the minimum space that would be economically viable. This can seat around 60 to 70 people. As demand grows, this can be replicated in other places in the same town. We had a lot of designs from the Indian Institute of Interior Designers. We are planning to go for all digital operations so that this can be scaled up at minimal time based on demand anywhere.

We had the first level demand assessment through two sources. We conducted a survey among the IT companies, where we asked them which cities they would like to have smaller facilities like this. We also had feedback from individuals working outside Kerala to see what kind of environment they are looking for and which cities they prefer. We have created the heat map of demand across Kerala. We start with the cities of higher demand and then go to the next cities in that order.

We are convinced that this is going to be the infrastructure facility for the current and future generations working in the knowledge economy. This will definitely help give a boost to the industry, stimulating growth, creating employment, and cost optimization for the users.

Reflections from Experts Across the World

Charles Edquist

I will raise a couple of issues that are a little more generic, that are related to the knowledge economy, and that are of relevance also for Kerala. The issues are highly relevant for the future of the knowledge economy in Kerala, particularly for policy actions that will be necessary to realize objectives in this field.

I want to place my comments in the context of what I call activities or functions in innovation systems. As I see it, these activities are the following:

1. R&D,
2. Education and training,
3. Formation of new product markets,
4. Articulation of quality requirement,
5. Creating and changing organizations,
6. Interactive learning,
7. Creating and changing institutions,
8. Incubation,
9. Financing of innovation processes, and
10. Consultancy services

These activities are the hypothetical determinants of the Development and the diffusion of innovations. Together, they may be said to define an innovation system.

Charles Edquist, Ruben Rausing Chair in Innovation Research at CIRCLE, Lund University, Sweden. **E-mail:** Charles.Edquist@circle.lu.se

This is a very wide definition of a system of innovation. It may be noted that policy is not a separate activity—but a part of all ten activities. Today, I want to deal briefly with two things that have been neglected very much in research and policy related to innovations, innovation systems, and innovation policy. One of these is education and training. In the literature on innovation systems, you will not find much about education and training. So, education and training are very important things to focus on—which you are obviously doing here in Kerala, as we have also heard from other speakers in this consultation.

But another thing that has also been highly neglected in innovation studies and innovation policy is the demand side. And that is number three and four in the list, i.e. "formation of new product markets" and "articulation of quality requirements".

Activities three and four include what I call functional public procurement. This is an enormously neglected issue in policies in the field of the knowledge economy and innovations in basically all countries of the world. Public procurement is around 15 per cent of the global GDP, i.e. an enormous sum. This means that public procurement is much more important than Global Research and Development (R&D). These enormous resources are being used by the public sector to buy things from private firms. This made me interested in how this could be used as a policy measure for getting more innovation dynamism in the economy. And I found out that this 15 per cent of GDP is almost not at all used to enhance innovations. The reason is that when public sector agencies buy things from the public sector, they describe a product, and they get the exact product. And it cannot be an innovation because you cannot describe an innovation—since it does not (yet) exist. What they should do instead is they should describe a problem that they want to solve by means of the products that they buy. If they describe a problem instead of a product, then they get many proposals for how that problem can be solved, and some of the proposals are innovations. This is potentially a very important thing. We argue that such functional procurement is potentially the most important public innovation policy instrument that can be used in all countries.

All the ten activities listed above: R&D, education, demand side, institutions, organization, and financing are all necessary for a dynamic innovation system to operate. From a policy-maker's point of view, it is a matter of identifying those activities that are not working well. If something is working very well, the policy-makers do not need to do anything about it and should instead concentrate on those things that are not working well.

Some people call this market failure. That is a too narrow term coming from economics, and I think it should be used in a wider sense. It could be called policy problems that should be addressed by innovation policy. That is being done to some extent. But in many cases, public policy is just duplicating what private actors are doing. And that is not needed. That is not a good use of resources. Public policy should be additional to what private actors are doing. In pursuing innovation policy, it is important to make a distinction between policy-makers and politicians. And it is the politicians who are pursuing innovation policies. I want to conclude by mentioning the establishment of a new kind of actor that has been created in Sweden: The National Innovation Council (NIC), chaired by the Prime Minister and including four additional ministers and ten external advisers.

Thank you very much.

Zhang Liyan

Hello everyone. The earlier presentations mainly discussed the theory part, but I would like to give some feedback on the practical aspects. I will share some institutional arrangements in China and propose some suggestions accordingly.

1. "Challenge Cup" Competition

About 30 years back, when the concept of venture capital came into China, the "Challenge Cup" National University Students Extracurricular Academic Technology Competition (hereinafter referred to as the "Challenge Cup" Competition) was co-sponsored by the Central Committee of the Communist Youth League, the Chinese Association for Science and Technology, the Ministry of Education, the All-China Federation of Students and local governments.

The "Challenge Cup" competition has two parallel projects in China: one is the "Challenge Cup" Chinese college student entrepreneurship plan competition, and the other is the "Challenge Cup" national college students' extracurricular academic technology competition. The national competitions of these two projects are carried out alternately, and each project is held every two years. Since the first competition was held in 1989, it has grown from 19 colleges/universities to more than 1,000 colleges/universities, with more than 2 million students participating each year.

Zhang Liyan, Professor and Director, Center for Innovation and Entrepreneurship, Tianjin University of Finance and Economics, China. **E-mail:** liyan_zhang_666@163.com

Achievements display, technology transfer, and technological entrepreneurship have brought the "Challenge Cup" competition from campus to society and promoted the transformation of scientific and technological achievements of colleges and universities into real productivity. "

2. "Internet+" Innovation and Entrepreneurship Competition

With the widespread penetration of the Internet into all aspects of the Chinese economy and the emergence of the importance of innovation and entrepreneurship, the China "Internet +" College Student Innovation and Entrepreneurship Competition was launched in 2015. As of 2019, a total of 9.47 million college students and 2.3 million teams participated in the five competitions, and a large number of high-quality projects with high technological content, large market potential, and good social benefits have emerged. According to the survey data of 528 projects that won the gold and silver awards in the previous four years, about half of the companies that established companies after the creative projects completed financing, and 19 per cent of the projects completed financing of more than 50 million yuan; the annual income of practical projects in 2018. The proportion of more than 50 million yuan is 13 per cent, and the annual revenue of the highest project exceeds 200 million yuan.

Since 2019, the Internet+ Contest has evolved from a national competition to an international one. In 2020, college student teams from 100-plus countries participated in the competition.

The sixth competition (2020) hosts a series of competitions for university students, vocational college students, and high school students. The poverty alleviation competition is also organized. The competition mainly adopts the three-level competition system of school-level preliminary competition, provincial semi-finals, and national finals. School-level preliminary competitions are organized by each school, provincial semi-finals are organized by localities, and national finals are selected and recommended according to the quota determined by the competition organizing committee.

3. Innovation and Entrepreneurship Platform

In China, every university/college has a maker space, and almost all the universities of science and engineering have science and technology parks. A university S&T park is more like a transitional entity between an incubator and a science and technology park, which is run by a company. In addition, all schools offer innovation and entrepreneurship courses in China.

4. Suggestions

Kerala is building a knowledge-based economy. An innovative ecosystem is critically important, and so is the involvement of university students, young people full of energy as they want to contribute to society. The challenge for the youth in China, India, and other countries is that they are far away from real society. Government organizations try to narrow the gap. Therefore, I'd like to propose three suggestions:

(1) *Organizing Innovation and Entrepreneurship Competitions*

Competition may become one of the solutions for building a knowledge-based economy. Organizing innovation and entrepreneurship competitions is a low-cost, quick-effective, highly-participated, and easy-to-manage activity.

At the same time, attracting companies to participate in the competitions. They will give the challenges they are facing to the students and let them provide solutions.

(2) *Providing Innovation and Entrepreneurship Training*

Innovation and Entrepreneurship training is to train people with the intention of starting a small business and small business managers in the aspects of business creation ability, market management quality etc. and give them certain policy guidance in the process of business establishment and operation.

(3) *Providing Platforms*

Innovation and entrepreneurship need a platform and an environment. The government needs to provide support to encourage colleges and universities to use existing facilities to set up maker spaces to offer courses. Both maker spaces and courses should be open to society.

Sushil Khanna

Skilling is needed for a knowledge economy. To go back on it, we have some very renowned international scholars. The focus here is to improve what we call the ecosystem. Here, we are looking at the educational skill level of a knowledge economy.

We should not focus too much on just digital issues or remote work and teaching. I think many of these trends will be short-term and reverse. I do think universities and everybody want to go back to the old face-to-face kind of thing. Offices will be working in a year or two, but I want to go back to the whole idea that Mr. Balagopal was talking about in the earlier session: that we need to have a system for high-tech manufacturing and high-tech production in Kerala.

Roughly, we have tracked about Rs. 4000 crore worth of shipment out of Kerala, high tech products and high tech is fined by OECD. What is high tech is that they have some HSN codes they call the high-tech industries. But Kerala, like in other products, has a huge deficiency in high-tech products, including aerospace and stuff like that must be going to ISRO.

But there is a great opportunity to enhance that sector, which requires new kinds of skills and new kinds of innovations. I will talk a little bit about the education system in Kerala. We have the highest literacy in this country. We have very good primary and secondary education, but Kerala has not been able to keep pace with the tertiary education. This is a major setback. I think it needs attention from the policy-makers.

Sushil Khanna, Professor, IIM, Kolkata, India. **E-mail:** sushil@iimcal.ac.in

Kerala has very few accredited colleges compared to your neighbours, for example, roughly 200-250 colleges. It has a disproportionately large number of enrollment. The higher education survey from 2011 to 2018 shows a sharp increase of 10-12 per cent in enrollment.

Some very interesting facts come up when you look at it. Firstly, the enrollment of women in undergraduate colleges is twice that of men, and in post-graduation education, it is three times higher. But very few women then get into the labour force, and more than 35 per cent of them stay out of the labour force and have a higher unemployment rate. There are only 9000 post-graduate students in Kerala, which I think is very small compared to Tamil Nadu and Karnataka. The State's population is double, but the number of accredited colleges is four times or five times higher. Post-graduate education is far more widespread. So, I think, the kind of skills that these colleges are imparting are disproportionate to what I want to call general education. While we do fairly well with respect to B.Ed., nursing, and the like, with respect to science, technology, and higher education, there is much to be desired. There are more than 100 engineering colleges. None of them are known nationally. So, there is a great need to improve the quality of higher education and tertiary education in Kerala. Then, there is also an opportunity for the large number of Kerala scholars spread all over the world and outside other universities in India, and there is an opportunity to attract them back.

There is a burst of new innovative industries, artificial intelligence. Industry entrepreneurs I met around Kochi were not the people who were returning from the Middle East. Most of them are Kerala NRIs from North America and Europe. Many of them have come back and started, and some are collaborating with their former employers in the USA and starting hardware production using artificial intelligence and advanced chemicals and stuff like that. So there is already been a small trend during the last five to ten years, and this needs to be strengthened. It needs a substantial improvement in the tertiary education. Kerala spends a lot of money on the Budget. All private colleges also get grants and support, but I think we need to use this support more judicially to push them towards getting better standards, to get accredited, to change the kind of courses and curriculum that they do, and so on.

Mammo Muchie

First and foremost, I give my great appreciation for Kerala. You are in a progressive state; you are doing many interesting things. The interesting thing now is that the digital world, the virtual world, is becoming universal. Even in agriculture, even if you do not know how to read and write, you can still use a mobile phone.

What does it mean to have digital skills? Do we do it through school or through otherwise? How we do it is a very interesting challenge. In other words, our people who are in agriculture can do digital agriculture. So are digital manufacturing and digital services. So, the skills, the reskilling, and the upscaling issue is a serious one.

I just want to tell you that in South Africa, I have been running a Technology venture creation course this semester, and I did it virtually. I formed the students into groups, and they created certain new venture start-ups. Also, I suggested they do not work on the previous activities but on the new ones, in other words, the sustainable Development, the green ones. Be innovators, inventors, creators of the venture, create start-ups, and things like that.

And then the idea is, I do not want the students to just get grades. By writing papers, I want them to do something practical. In other words, they produce some venture. I must tell you what one of the groups did. The initial seed capital they needed was not available. Sometimes, if they did not get it, they used to get some support from my networks. But you know what they did? They sold

---

Mammo Muchie, DST/NRF Research Professor, Faculty of Management Sciences, Tshwane University of Technology, South Africa.

E-mail: mammo.muchie@gmail.com, muchiem@tut.ac.za

their cars and started building their own venture start-ups. Can you imagine something like that happening now?

So, an interesting time is on us. So, what I would like to do is that even the courses we are developing now, we are thinking of making it global virtually because when we do it virtually, it is possible that the whole world can join our courses. So, I am now thinking about how I can motivate my university to see if we can make it next time. So that all of you could get involved. So, I like some collaboration, very genuine collaboration, where all our students, if they are all engineering students and they are all interesting students, and they are all motivated, and I like us to develop some new skills, and it is where we collaborate. And I think Kerala can come into this picture, and I think we could do that. The other interesting thing is what our Professor Charles Edquist said about the concept of the holistic Innovation system. I am not interested in a national innovation system since, in the digital world, there is no boundary; boundaries are finished! As humans are becoming machines, machine learning is more important.

All activities are changing, and the work world is also changing. The speakers also put it how many new jobs are created that are digital. Things are different for the physical world and the physical work; what we used to do is changing dramatically. Our classrooms are changing, and what would be very interesting now is the innovation system should be developed more with the theory of unassigned.

And there is a loss of jobs for our young people; we must be careful because if you lose jobs, unemployment comes, poverty comes, and inequality comes, it means danger comes. For people, many risks come, like environmental challenges, many things. So, to avoid it, we need to rethink the innovation system by using what I really like what Charles Edquist said, the concept of a holistic innovation system. I prefer to call it differently. The social innovator.

Let's get a few more names. Earlier, we used to have regional and local innovation systems etc. Let's move from geography to the social world, the unified world. The validation criteria should not be economics, economics for profit alone is not good. What does it do? When you create some jobs, you lose some jobs, and you create sociological loss. We must make a win-win link. Some new approach, some new vision, some new idea.

I must tell you, I call Kerala my homeland. I must say that from all the progressive things you have been doing. Can I just challenge you now? Now, with this digital knowledge economy, you create a new innovation system. The new concept, the holistic one, the social one, the social innovation system, not the local Kerala innovation system or anything like that, or the Indian innovation system. Let's move towards that. Let's change. I am saying to rethink. Unthink to rethink, unlearn to relearn, un-engineer to re-engineer, un-science to re-science, and un-economics to re-economics. So, we are in a new world. Going for the new world. Kerala,

Thank you so much.

Thank you, all of you.

Glenda Kruss

I shall begin by raising a few points in comparison with policy processes in South Africa that we are grappling with and similar to that of Kerala. After 1994, South Africa moved towards a democratic government. In 1996, we adopted a new STI policy that foregrounded the knowledge economy and the national system of innovation. In 2019, we designed a new white paper that sets out the framework within which we are working with policy instruments and mechanisms and so on. Our policy aims to promote innovation for inclusive and sustainable development that promotes transformation in society, and we also have foregrounded the fourth industrial revolution. Our presidential commission has submitted its completed report in December 2020.

There are a lot of parallels with the processes in Kerala. Our presidential commission has also foregrounded the investment in human capital and highlighted the need to design, streamline, and align our education system through a coordinated multi-stakeholder process. What is happening here today in Kerala is such a coordinated multi-stakeholder process. Very different from what you have said about Kerala, where you have a problem of unemployed graduates and skilled professionals. In South Africa, we have a large pool of unemployed who do not have the right kinds of skills for the new kinds of jobs. I am making that point to compare some of the strategies we are adopting.

Over the past four or five months, I have been involved in a province to develop the economic and social development strategy, and we are part of a panel that is developing our housing strategy, and central to that is skills. I just wanted

---

Glenda Kruss, Research Director at HSRC, South Africa. **E-mail:** gkruss@hsrc.ac.za

to share two points that came up in our strategy. One is that we need to develop our paradigm and our framework for thinking about skills development. We have a framework for Economic Development, and then we elaborate that into thinking about our skills development.

We have also identified high-growth industry sectors like you have in Kerala, but slightly different. Apart from ICT and digital services, food, beverages, agro-processing, and agro-businesses, we have also highlighted sectors such as cultural and creative services and the cannabis industry. But then what I thought could be quite useful to insert into the discussion here is the groupings of the types of skills that we need to grow.

There is a big list of the types of skills that need to be developed in Kerala. In our strategy, we have grouped these into four. One is the technology skills related to physical, digital, and biological dimensions. So, we need to develop advanced digital skills to design, develop, and support our technologies that are underpinning new ways of doing things. But what is equally important is the societal dimension and the digital society. In that regard, we need to make sure that we are developing the right skills so that people can thrive in the workplace of the future. But equally in the business skills, the business dimension is critical. So, we see the omnipresence of digitalization, the need for digital trust, and the need for new models.

So, we need to develop new skills to take advantage of new ways of managing and doing business, and that is equally important. And then, finally, at the governance level, we need new kinds of policy new regulation, and we need to be ready to respond to the new opportunities and demands of globalization as being stressed here today. Hence, we need to develop skill development programmes. We have to include governance skills to take into account rapidly changing technology in an increasingly global world.

The second point I wanted to make is about the nature of teaching and learning. The example that I wanted to talk about is a proposal for our skills development that enabled apprenticeships in South Africa. I know that the Kerala strategy talks a lot about technical and vocational education and financial commitment to apprenticeships. In South Africa, we typically have our apprenticeships focusing on theoretical knowledge, practical skills, and workplace experience. The way that we do is very different because of technology and innovation and because of the innovations that we need in business models and processes. So, for example, we have open courses that use blended learning accessed from global universities.

We can use digital portfolios for data-informed decision-making. Blockchain gives us new tools for accreditation. We have got new tools for digital identification and authentication and so on. These technologies could support multiple learning pathways. I just want to point out that besides those three aspects traditionally of theoretical knowledge, practical skills, and workplace experience, we actually need new kinds of skills to be developed. To enable apprenticeships, life skills become much more important, and we need to extend that training to include critical life skills like financial literacy, psycho-social support etc. Particularly if you are going to be talking about working from home and working near home, we need to extend that training to include digital skills. So, in a country like South Africa, perhaps less so in Kerala, we need to skill young people very much in the use of advanced technologies in the workplace, digital safety, cyber security etc.

There is a need to extend our training to include entrepreneurship skills. So, if we have high levels of self-employment, we young people come up with skills in business management and, financial management etc. I must say I was so impressed with the depth of the planning that you had, which is evident from the excellent budget speech. Very clear planning in terms of numbers and approaches, and that is something we envy. We are trying to build our capacity to use digital means for more effective skills planning. I think that to deepen the process and going forward, it is very important to theorize and conceptualize a bit more tightly how it is linked with the framework for the economic growth strategy and how our skills Development itself can use digital means to deepen what is possible. Thank you, colleagues, and we look forward to engaging with you; if it were valid, we would love to engage through this state-level process to compare how we are grappling with these very similar challenges in significantly similar but different contexts.

Thank you.

Dinesh Abrol

The two points that I have not so far are one, the "who-whom" of the knowledge economy, and two, the guiding notions of the knowledge economy in use by professionals and policy-makers. Professor Khanna reminded us not to reduce knowledge to digital. The "who-whom" of the outcomes or the use values being gained needs to objectively assess the possible contribution of the digital economy in the making. The contribution of IT-enabled services is catering to our own economy in a limited way. They are upgrading the US or UK economy. And the workforce has remained confined to low-value-added activities. While the significance of high-tech activities is well understood, the outcomes need a critical evaluation. Take the investment in very large-scale integration (VLSI) design activity going on in Bangalore. India has not been able to create a high-tech economy due to the lack of investment in the required complementary manufacturing activities. Is the state government in a position to bring such complementary investments to Kerala?

Prof. Khanna drew our attention to the transient nature of trends like working from home, online education, and other such services. However, we have opportunities and potential in the possibilities of upgrading the system of resources and knowledge of economic and medicinal plants. There is the possibility of upgrading the manufacturing capabilities associated with the Development of traditional health systems. We have opportunities in the services and tourism industry as well. Kerala will have to invest in the local system of education and competence building to further develop these resources and capabilities; a higher priority to the building of spaces for interactive learning

---

Dinesh Abrol, Professor, Jawaharlal Nehru University, New Delhi.

E-mail: dinesh.abrol@gmail.com

to attain transformative innovation outcomes is the positive answer. This will ensure that the benefits are not confined to just a small section of the upper echelons of the middle class.

The challenge of developing local resources and capabilities requires the relevant actors to co-produce knowledge and co-design solutions. System development rather than heroic approaches is the way forward. But the process of formulation of science, technology, and innovation policy (STIP, 2020) has completely bypassed the states. The STIP 2020 draft available for public discussion has been worked out without interacting with the states. A progressive government is in place in Kerala, and it is expected to make investments in science, technology, and innovation to serve the people. In the given context, the question is how the state government of Kerala should be investing in the local system of education and competence building to enhance the absorptive capacity of the State and formulate policy programmes for the upgrading of the knowledge economy of Kerala.

The progressive tradition of promotion of collective action in Kerala is her strength. Local self-government capacity for the benefit of people's planning has been attempted in Kerala. Kudumbshree, the largest woman solidarity and social economy programme in the world, is in place in the State of Kerala. How is the state government planning to link these components of the existing ecosystem with the upgrading of the knowledge economy? How can the state government encourage these strengths to actively participate in the Development of the Knowledge Economy?

There are the challenges of climate change requiring distributed capabilities but networked to undertake disaster management. Health and environmental challenges require the knowledge economy to contribute to building on the resilience shown during the COVID-19 crisis. Information and communication technology (ICT) skills and capabilities need to be harnessed for the benefit of disaster management and climate risk reduction. Can Kerala harness the ICT skills and competencies to develop unique strengths and become the source of knowledge and capabilities? Can we create a platform economy for the benefit of providing producer services for climate risk reduction and agricultural services? In Kerala, the Knowledge Economy should be connected with the processes of people planning and the Development of the role and contribution of local self-governments. Let us innovate to create a universal basic infrastructure capable of a sustainable urban economy.

The vibrant local self-governments can enable the social cooperatives to develop as social carriers of a circular economy in Kerala. Development of the nodes of a networked system of group enterprises is also the key to the Development of universal basic infrastructure and a pro-people platform economy. Kerala should not be in the hands of Uber and Ola, Monsanto and Bayer, and so on. The private parties could participate and contribute by following the rules of the game to be determined democratically. The notion of innovation has been misused and abused to capture the direction of the development process, and so also the notions of knowledge economy and knowledge society. Whose knowledge should count is not an unimportant question. Kerala can provide leadership in mobilizing the higher and secondary education system to participate in the tasks of mapping, analysis, planning, and implementation activities. All over the world, there are models available for the integration of education and economy, and we should be open to their import. However, we should be evaluating the "who-whom" of the proposed models.

Edward Henry Lorenz

Introduction

In reading for a second time the 2021-22 Budget Speech of Kerala's Finance Minister, Dr. Thomas Issac, I was struck again by its breadth and the extent to which it focuses on building the knowledge-based economy in Kerala in combination with social inclusiveness. The Budget Speech addresses a wide range of policies related to this goal, including measures to address unemployment and strengthen social security, promote job creation and start-ups, provide training, and support higher education reform. Moreover, the speech sets out industrial support policies for both high-tech sectors and traditional handicrafts.

Below, I offer some reflections on the skills and job impacts of the 4th Industrial Revolution (4IR) and on policies for training and skills development that may have a bearing on constructing Kerala's inclusive knowledge-based economy. A difficulty in undertaking policy-relevant research on the 4IR is the very limited amount of micro-level data that has been collected on the adoption of these technologies, including AI and robotics, which have been identified as technologies that could have a big negative effect on jobs and employment. Early estimates by Frey and Osborne (2013) predicted that 47 per cent of employees in the US were at high risk of having their jobs eliminated within a decade or so, and a report by the World Bank (2016) using the same methodology predicted similarly alarming impacts on jobs in developing countries, with the figure

Edward Henry Lorenz, University of Johannesburg and University of Aalborg.
E-mail: ned.lorenz@gmail.com

for India put at slightly over 40 per cent after adjusting for a time lag due to relatively low labour costs. It has now become clear that these predictions were exaggerated, and a recent World Economic Forum report (2020) argues that the number of jobs created will outpace those destroyed. In recent McKinsey reports (2018), the focus is more on the changing skills requirements of existing occupations due to automation than on the wholesale elimination of occupations.

The Importance of Micro and Small Enterprises

The estimates referred to above are based either on aggregate data or on surveys of relatively small samples of larger and mostly multinational companies. This research does not consider possible firm heterogeneity in the impact of 4IR technologies, including differences due to scale or size. As micro-level data on 4IR technology adoption has progressively become available, it shows that there are important differences between micro, small, and medium enterprises (MSMEs) compared to larger firms, both in terms of adoption rates and types of new technologies used. For example, a study based on a survey of 4IR technology adoption in manufacturing in several EU counties identified a positive relation between the scale of production and batch size on the one hand and the intensity of adoption of industrial robots on the other (Dachs and Palčič, 2020). The recent EU-wide enterprise survey of AI use similarly identifies higher rates of adoption amongst large firms compared to micro and small firms, and it also identifies differences in how AI is integrated with micro-enterprises relying more on purchased software ready-to-use as compared to large enterprises, which more frequently develop AI fully in-house. (European Commission, 2020). Research that I have been engaged in with Erika Kraemer Mbula and others using the results of the survey carried out in 2019 of digital technology adoption in a sample of micro and small firms, including informal businesses, in the Johannesburg region of South Africa, shows virtually no adoption of many of the technologies that figure prominently in the literature on the 4IR such integrated business management system based on artificial intelligence and big data analytics. What the Johannesburg survey results do show is that micro firms are adopting several affordable digital technologies and tools that are adapted to their scale, such as social media, data storage on the cloud, and browsing the Internet to access information and ideas for developing new products and services. We find a statistically significant relation between the use of social media on the one hand and product innovation on the other (Gaglio *et al.*, 2021).

These insights on the distinctive technology adoption patterns of MSMEs are relevant to the discussion on the adoption of 4IR in Kerala, given the importance of the MSME sector. The Indian Government's 2020-21 Annual Report on MSMEs estimated the number of MSMEs in Kerala at 44.6 lakh, the large majority of which are both micro and informal businesses. MSMEs account for about 40 per cent of total employment in Kerala, and over 50 per cent of MSMEs are located in rural areas. As the report observes, MSMEs play a crucial role by providing large employment opportunities at comparatively lower capital costs, and they help to reduce regional imbalances (Annual Report, 2020-21, p. 23). One implication that follows from this is the importance of investing in adequate digital infrastructure and increasing the level of access to the Internet. In terms of a standard measure of internet access, the number of internet subscribers per 100 population, Kerala at 71.3 per 100 population in 2019, performed well compared to India as a whole at 52.1. There remains, however, a big rural/urban divide in Kerala, with the subscription figures for rural and urban being respectively 37.7 and 171.2 subscriptions per 100 population (TRAI, 2020). The K-FON project discussed in the Finance Minister's speech which aims to provide free internet access to all BPL families and to assure interoperability arguably will be crucial to constructing the knowledge-based economy in Kerala and improving MSME innovation performance.

Vocation Education and Training for an Inclusive Knowledge-based Society

Another issue that has been widely discussed by both economists and policy-makers is identifying the skills that are needed for the digital-based knowledge economy. The Budget Speech put an emphasis on higher education and STEM skills, including those specific to 4IR technologies such as data analytics, artificial intelligence, and robotic process automation. These high-level skills are of undoubted importance. However, it is also important to balance measures designed to increase the quality and supply of STEM skills with investments in the initial technical vocational education and training (TVET) system to increase the supply of mid and lower-level technical and operational skills. One reason for doing this is to construct an inclusive society in which all youth have the opportunity to pursue a career that offers the potential for secure employment and upgrading over time. The simple fact is that even in the most developed European economies, it is rare that more than 50 per cent of the relevant age cohort attain university-level education. An inclusive society will be as much concerned about those youth not pursuing a higher-level university degree as those that do. In many cases in Europe, the share of youth attending university is much lower. In Germany, which is often described as Europe's industrial powerhouse, in 2018, only slightly more than 30 per cent of the 30-to-35-year age cohort that had completed their formal initial education had a higher-level university degree. Instead of choosing full-time academic education, a much larger share of youth had opted for Germany's dual apprenticeship system, where school leavers, usually at the age of 16, take up a vocational apprenticeship combining training in the workplace with alternating periods of formal classroom training in a technical college. Since apprenticeship qualifications are recognized nationally in Germany and offer opportunities for upgrading one's career, the vocational track is perceived positively by a majority of youth.

Skills Development for Learning Organisations

Investing in the initial TVET system will be central to constructing an inclusive society that offers a viable future for all youth, including school leavers. It is increasingly being recognized, however, that there is value in integrating a workplace-based training component into educational tracks at all levels of the system, including tertiary-level university education. For example, the French higher-level university system at the Master level now systematically offers the option of 'alternate' in which students alternate between formal classroom education at the university and working in an enterprise. This is designed in part to bridge the gap in relevance that students typically experience between the codified academic knowledge imparted in the classroom and the more practical and firm-specific knowledge they need to perform their jobs. Further, by reducing problems of skills mismatch, it also aims to increase the employability of more highly educated youth. Kerala's Additional Skills Acquisition Programme (ASAP), initiated in 2012, is a good example of a transformative educational programme that can serve these goals.

Combining formal classroom education and practical work experience at all levels of the educational system relates to a broader distinction that Bengt-Aake Lundvall and I, with others, have developed between STI (science, technology, and innovation) mode learning and innovation based on codified knowledge and DUI (doing, using and interacting) mode learning and innovation based largely on tacit knowledge acquired through working experience. Based on an empirical study of the Danish economy, we provided evidence that the two modes are complementary, and we showed that firms that combine the two modes are more likely to succeed at innovation than firms that emphasize one or the other mode (Jensen *et al.*, 2007). Work-study programmes of the sort offered through the French system of 'alternate' will increase the preparedness of the enterprise to bring together the two modes of learning and innovation and benefit from their complementarities.

Moreover, since many of the most important skills for innovation will be acquired over time at the workplace, it will be important to organize work activity in the firm in a way that offers employees opportunities for ongoing learning and problem-solving. This will be the case even for the skills employees need to work with new 4IR technologies such as artificial intelligence. With colleagues at the Aalborg University Business School, I recently contributed to designing a questionnaire for an employee-level survey measuring skills and AI use that was carried out by Statistics Denmark in 2019 on a random sample of 1244 private sector employees. Over 40 per cent of the employees who make use of AI in their daily work activities ranked the training they had received at the workplace from peers, such as experienced colleagues, as being as important or more important for acquiring the skills they need for working with AI than formal classroom training (Gjerding *et al.,* 2020). This, of course, does not mean that firms can afford to forego investing in the high-level skills of the data and software engineers who are responsible for designing and implementing AI systems in the enterprise. The majority of employees, however, will not need these high-level programming skills. Being effective in their jobs will require the level of digital literacy needed to utilize a variety of digital devices (e.g., computers, smartphones, tablets) and to work with various digital interfaces (e.g., e-mail, internet, social media). As our research has shown, an important avenue for acquiring this level of digital literacy will be ongoing learning on the job.

REFERENCES

Annual Report, 2020-21, Ministry of Micro, Small and Medium Enterprises, Udyog Bhavan, New Delhi-110011.

Dachs, B. and I. Palčič (2020). "Not for Everybody? Product Characteristics and Digital Production Technologies in Manufacturing Firms", *Review d'EconomieIndustrielle,* pp. 37-56.

European Commission, (2020). "European enterprise survey on the use of technologies based on artificial intelligence", A Study Prepared for the European Commission by IPSOS Belgium and the Solvay Brussels School of Economics and Management.

Frey, C.B. and Osborne, M.A. (2017). "The future of employment: How susceptible are jobs to computerization?", *Technological Forecasting and Social Change, 114,* 254-80.

Gaglio, C., E. Kraemer-Mbula and E. Lorenz (2021). "Innovation, Digitization, and Productivity in South African Micro and Small Enterprises", Paper accepted for Presentation at the 2021 Globelics Conference, Costa Rica.

Gjerding, A., J. Rubæk Holm, E. Lorenz and J. Stamhus (2020). "Ready, but challenged: Diffusion and Use of Artificial Intelligence and Robotics in Danish Firms", Aalborg University Business School Working Paper.
McKinsey Global Institute (2018). "Skill shift. Automation and the Future of Work".
TRAI (2020). Telecom Regulatory Authority of India", *The Indian Telecom Services Performance Indicators*, July—September 2019.
World Bank (2016). *World Bank Development Report.*
World Economic Forum (2020). *The Future of Jobs Report.*

Anna Kingiri

My presentation is going to focus on a few lessons for knowledge development and diffusion and how this can enhance our national innovation system. I would like to draw some lessons from M-Pesa innovation, which is a mobile money service in Kenya, very popular in Kenya, and is also being used in East Africa and other parts of Africa. Of course, questions have been asked why this mobile money service has been successful in Kenya but not in other countries. For those who are aware, this is a service that was introduced in 2007 and to date, it has revolutionized the operations not just in the financial sector, but also in other operational sectors in Kenya. When it was introduced, it was targeted at inclusive financial access, particularly by the grassroots communities. Some of the lessons that I would want to share I would imagine that they would also be useful for other sectors that are critical for Kerala. Like the renewable energy sector, biotechnology sector, and, of course, other sectors within the Fourth Industrial Revolution.

The very first factor that has been found to be very critical in Kenya for the development of dynamic technological innovation like M-Pesa, is that there is a new need to consider the aspect of product development. And of course, these would relate to a number of areas, but mainly to research and development. This is very critical. The other factor has to do with our development of the market-related innovation. This particular aspect of innovation has been associated with incremental innovation, the need to build the capacity of entrepreneurs, and the need to build the skills of young innovators which in turn contributed in a great way to the growth of M-Pesa in Kenya.

Anna Kingiri, African Centre for Technology Studies, Nairobi, Kenya.
E-mail: anna ankingiri@gmail.com

The other area that is very critical is the aspect of product development that is driven by continuous adaptation that users demand. And of course, this is key to process innovation. But more important is learning and capabilities development; regardless of being a grassroots actors, SMEs, or academic institutions. The capacities and learning must be commensurate to the needs of both the technology developers, as well as the uses of the technology. This is yet another factor found to have driven the growth of M-Pesa.

The other aspect that I think is very critical for the Kenyan case is policy innovation, where the government has contributed in a very large way to the promotion of, young innovators and young entrepreneurs. This has been found to have supported the ICT curriculum development across different sectors and also in the development of a supportive STI policy that promotes the other areas that have been found to be quite critical for the growth of M-Pesa. It ensures resources for R&D, market innovation and research, and for policy innovation.

Finally, for a functional technological innovation system, it has been found that policy should actually support the factors that target system failure. That is something that has been very critical for the Kenyan digital innovation. It has been found that these areas must change to their capacity and the skills needed by the different states. Therefore, technologists, as well as the developers of the technology must consider skills and capacities. So, I believe some of the factors that contributed to the growth of M-Pesa could be of relevance in the transformation of Kerala to become a knowledge economy. I do hope that the policy-makers as well as the researchers can draw from the success of M-Pesa and inform our discussions and conversations.

Thank you.

Part III

Towards a Way Forward

Knowledge, Innovation and Sustainable and Inclusive Development

Reflections from Cuba

Aurora Fernández-González

Introduction

The Kerala government's vision of transforming Kerala into a knowledge economy is of great interest to the countries of the South. The goals of sustainable and inclusive development demand the strengthening of educational, scientific, and technological capacities. In Cuba, great efforts have been made for decades to strengthen the connections between knowledge, innovation, and development. The aim of this contribution is to comment on three issues that from our experience are of great importance: (1) the role of the university and its social projection; (2) the importance of having advanced technological capacities in strategic sectors for the country, such as health; and (3) the role of public policies and government action in promoting innovation systems.

Each of these topics is discussed briefly below and, at the end, the connections between them are shown through an example related to vaccines against COVID-19.

Aurora Fernández-González, Adviser to the Minister of Higher Education, Cuba, Jorge Núñez-Jover, University of Havana. **E-mail:** aurorafg@gmail.com

The University-Society Relationship as a Primordial Issue

The university-society relationship has occupied an important place in the Latin American university tradition since the Cordoba Reform (1918) and has been extensively debated in the Regional Conferences on Higher Education in Latin America and the Caribbean (LAC) (1996, 2008, 2018) (Núñez, 2019, pp. 67-77). It is recognised that in Latin America and the Caribbean, universities are key actors in science, technology, and innovation systems (Castro-Martínez and Sutz, 2010).

The social relevance of the university is a fundamental value in Cuban higher education and occupies a preferential place in the evaluation and accreditation systems of universities and in the promotion processes of professors and researchers. This approach influences the orientation of research and innovation activities. According to the UNESCO Science Report 2021 (UNESCO, 2021, p. 20) in the context of the pandemic, "mission-oriented research" has increased. It states that LAC has been a pioneer in this approach and that Europe is moving in this direction.

In Cuba such an approach is usual. The antecedents date back to the 1962 University Reform, which defined scientific research as an inherent characteristic of the university. Since the mid-1960s, this research has been increasingly oriented towards the solution of problems of social practice.

The orientation towards innovation was accentuated from the late 1980s and early 1990s with the creation of research centres in various universities, in the areas of new materials, and medical equipment, among others (Pérez and Núñez, 2009).

In the last 5 years, several universities have created science and technology parks, companies, and foundations, which aim to foster links between universities and the goods and productive sectors.

The role of our universities in local development is very important and relatively new. The Constitution of the Republic of 2019 (National Assembly of People's Power, 2019) declares the autonomy of municipalities. However, this autonomy requires capacity building in the territories. In most municipalities, there are municipal university centres, closely linked to the major universities and research centres. The municipal university centres expand university-society links and offer the possibility of connecting knowledge, innovation and development at the community level (Díaz-Canel and Fernández, 2020).

High Technology and Inclusive Health Systems

Cuba has a well-developed biotechnology-medical-pharmaceutical industry (Núñez and Figueroa, 2017; Núñez *et al.*, 2011) that began to take off in the 1980s and since 2012 has been grouped into the state business organisation BioCubaFarma, which brings together 32 companies, supplies more than 800 products to the health system—including 349 drugs from the basic list—owns 182 patent objects, carries out more than 100 simultaneous clinical trials with its products at 200 clinical sites and has exported its products to more than 50 countries. These centres carry out scientific research, technological development, production and export activities.

The industry is well articulated with health programmes aimed at the entire Cuban population. Among the many products it has created are vaccines of notable national and international impact, such as the vaccine against meningococcal meningitis type B, the recombinant vaccine against hepatitis B virus, and the first synthetic vaccine for human use in the world: the vaccine against ImmunoInflenzae type B (Hib) produced by the University of Havana in collaboration with a group from Canada (Herrera, 2021).

More than 80 per cent of the vaccines that Cuban children receive free of charge are produced in Cuba.

It can be said that the Cuban biotechnology development model has been successful from scientific, social, and economic points of view (Lage, 2008).

Public Policy and Government Action

In Cuba, there is a strong tradition of direct participation of the highest levels of state and government in the orientation of science, technology, and innovation policies. The accelerated creation of the institutional foundations of national science in the 1960s and 1970s, as well as the origin and deployment of the biotechnology industry in the following two decades, illustrate this participation.

Science, technology, and innovation currently occupy a preferential place in the country's development agenda. Cuba has a national economic and social development plan until 2030 in which the production and use of knowledge is a priority. One of the strategic axes of this plan is called Human Potential, Science, Technology and Innovation. The current Constitution of the Republic is very emphatic in its formulation of the role of science and technology in national development.

STI policies in Cuba have been characterised by their strong social orientation, and by the human values that have driven them.

The management of such a policy has traditionally been in the hands of a ministry. However, the innovation systems approach teaches us that innovation is a process that requires connections between many actors and different sectors. To boost innovation policy, in May of this year the National Innovation Council, chaired by the President of the Republic, was created.

Innovation is now more prominent in public policy efforts in STI: the traditional emphasis on research has given way to innovation as a priority.

Cuban higher education has had for decades links with networks such as Globelics, LALICS and with theoretical elaborations coming from Latin American scholars [Dutrénit and Sutz, eds. (2014); Lastres, H. *et al.* (2005); Arocena and Sutz (2020)]. This has influenced Cuba to adopt innovation systems approaches in their broad sense [Lundvall, B.Å.; Joseph, K.; Chaminade, K.; Vang, C. (2009)], which are oriented towards sustainable and inclusive development and serve as a basis for public policy in STI.

The Context of the Pandemic

The direct involvement of the highest levels of government in science, technology and innovation issues through direct and systematic dialogue with groups of researchers and experts has paid off in the battle against the pandemic.

It has facilitated the identification of priorities, and the allocation of material and human resources and has strengthened the connections between the various actors, which has allowed much faster progress in solving problems. In particular the development of new technologies, for example, 2 vaccines and 3 other vaccine candidates against COVID-19, as well as the production of other innovative drugs, equipment, reagents, various inputs, and individual means of protection, among others (Martínez *et al.*, 2020).

One of these vaccines has been named Soberana 2 and is the result of collaboration between a research group at the University of Havana and BioCubaFarma's Finlay Vaccine Institute. The director of the Finlay Vaccine Institute, Vicente Vérez-Bencomo, is the same scientist who decades ago led Hib vaccine research at the University of Havana.

This example reveals the importance of the social responsibility of universities and their participation in the innovation system. It shows the importance of having their own technological capacities in strategic sectors such as human health. It also highlights the role of government management in creating a favourable institutional environment that foster connections between actors.

Conclusion

The point we have sought to emphasize is that sustainable and inclusive development requires the strengthening of knowledge and innovation capacities. The Cuban experience, particularly in the context of the pandemic, highlights the importance of three elements: (1) It is essential to have universities with research capacity, capable of engaging in innovation processes, (2) It is essential to develop advanced technological capacities in strategic sectors of great economic and social importance, and (3) Public policies and government action are decisive in promoting innovation.

REFERENCES

Arocena, R. &Sutz, J. (2020). "The need for new theoretical conceptualizations on National Systems of Innovation, based on the experience of Latin America", *Economics of Innovation and New Technology*, doi: 10.1080/10438599.2020.1719640. Available at: https://www.tandfonline.com/doi/abs/10.1080/10438599.2020.1719640

Asamblea Nacional del Poder Popular (ANPP). (2019). Constitución de la República de Cuba. GOC-2019-406-Ex 5.

Castro-Martínez, E. y Sutz, J. (2010). Universidad, conocimiento e innovación, pp. 102-119. En M. Albornoz y J. A. López Cerezo (eds.), Ciencia, tecnología y universidad en Iberoamérica. Buenos Aires: OEI, Eudeba

Díaz-Canel, M. y Fernández, A. (2020). "Gestión de gobierno, educación superior, ciencia, innovación y desarrollo local". *Retos de la Dirección*, *14*(2): 5-32, ISSN 2306-9155. Available at: https://revistas.reduc.edu.cu/index.php/retos/article/view/3571/3269

Dutrénit, G. y Sutz, J. (Ed.) (2014). *National Innovation Systems, Social Inclusion and Development*, Books, Edward Elgar Publishing, number 15491.

Herrera, L. (2021). "Cuba buscó una apuesta segura, con base en las posibilidades y en tecnología dominada". *Entrevista realizada para Cubadebate*, 12 April 2021 Ciencia y Tecnología, Cuba, Especiales, Salud. Available at: http://www.cubadebate.cu/especiales/2021/04/12/

Lage, Agustin. (2008). "Connecting immunology research to public health: Cuban biotechnology". *Nature Immunology*. *9*. 109-12. 10.1038/ni0208-109.

Lastres, H. *et al.* (2005). Conhecimento, sistemas de inovação e desenvolvimento. Río de Janeiro: Editora UFRJ; Contraponto.

Lundvall, B.Å., Joseph, K., Chaminade y K. y Vang, C. (2009). Innovation system research and developing countries, pp. 1-32. In Bengt-Åke Lundvall, K. J. Joseph, C. Chaminade J. Vang (eds.), *Handbook of Innovation Systems and Developing countries. Building Domestic Capabilities in a Global Setting*. Cheltenham, UK; Northampton, MA, USA: Edward Elgar Publishing. ISBN 978-1-84720-609.

Martínez, E., Pérez, R., Herrera, L., Lage, A. y Castellanos, L. (2020). "La industria biofarmacéutica cubana en el combate contra la pandemia de COVID-19". *Anales de la Academia de Ciencias de Cuba*, Vol. 10, No. 2: Special COVID-19.

Núñez, J. (2019). Conocimiento, universidad y desarrollo: nuevas encrucijadas. Una lectura desde Ciencia, Tecnología y Sociedad. Editorial UH 128 pp. ISBN 978-959-7251-45-3.

Núñez, J., Pérez, I. y Montalvo, L. (2011). Biotechnology, University and Scientific and Technological Policy in Cuba: A Look at Progress and Challenges. In *Biotechnology and Innovation Systems. The Role of Public Policy.* Göransson, B. y Pålsson, C.M. (editors), International Development Research Centre, Ottawa, ISBN 978-1-55250-538-0, pp.80-107

Núñez, J. y Figueroa, G. (2017). "University, Technology and Development: Reflections from the South [on line]". In B. Laspra, J.A. López Cerezo (eds.), *Spanish Philosophy of Technology*. Available at: https://link.springer.com/book/10.1007/978-3-319-71958-0#toc.

Pérez, I. y Núñez, J. (2009). "Higher Education and Socioeconomic Development in Cuba: High Rewards of a Risky High-Tech Strategy", *Science and Public Policy, 36*(2), March, pp 97-101.

UNESCO (2021). *Science Report 2021: The Race Against Time for Smarter Development,* UNESCO, Paris.

Reflections from Experts Across the World

Luc Soete

The most striking feature of Kerala highlighted in the Budget and which received much attention in the discussion is the highly educated labour force in Kerala. At first sight, it made me think of Richard Freeman's much-acclaimed book of 1976 the "*Overeducated American*".[1] A book which led to a lot of discussion in the United States and was more or less proven wrong subsequently. But let me quote from Dr. Isaac's Budget Speech: "Unemployment of the educated is the biggest developmental challenge faced by Kerala. The present employment schemes are inadequate to resolve unemployment of the educated."

So clearly there is something like the "Overeducated Keralite". But (s) he (she might be even more appropriate) looks today more like the successful outcome of Jan Tinbergen's [2] "race between education and technology" in favour of education. If the race is won by technology as it did in most rich countries, inequality would increasetechnological change, increasing the demand for more skilled workers.[3]

If like in Kerala, the race is won by education, the outcome could indeed result in an overeducated workforce with relatively limited income inequality. However, as an outcome, this is one that most policy-makers in the world would only dream about. It is an outcome that makes Kerala probably the best-placed economy in the world today to win the next «digital» Tinbergen race: to outperform the speed at which a whole range of new digital technologies,

Luc Soete, Professorial Fellow, UNU MERIT, Formerly Rector Magnificus of Maastricht University, Netherlands. **E-mail:** soete@merit.unu.edu

including artificial intelligence, are likely to be impacting today and in the near future all sectors in society.

In short, the overeducated Keralite is actually the main guarantee for Kerala to become over this decennium one of the most advanced digital economies and knowledge societies in the world.

It will though, as highlighted in Dr. Isaac's budget speech, require some specific policy action to exploit this specific higher education comparative advantage. First and foremost, addressing the high levels of unemployment of highly educated females; second, raising the quality of higher education; third, paying attention to the need for continuous technological upskilling and life-long learning (the Tinbergen race is never over…); fourth, invest in the availability of IT equipment and accessibility of IT infrastructure for all. A broad spectrum of actions is needed.

A second factor complementary to the overeducated Keralite, consists of attracting (foreign) capital to Kerala. It is a factor that again has been given a lot of attention in Dr. Isaac's budget speech with the creation amongst others of the K-DISC, the Start-up Mission, the Kerala Innovation Challenge, the S.B Sen Innovation fund, a venture capital fund and even paying particular attention to the remittances of non-resident Keralites. So, one can only encourage the Kerala government to be creative with measures activating capital, both based on public funds, domestically generated private savings, and foreign capital.

In conclusion, I quote from the last 2006 Globelics slide:

> Knowledge sharing… shifts the attention away from the purely technological aspects of research to the broader organisational, economic and social aspects which are today in many cases a more important factor behind innovation, than the technological ones.
>
> This holds a *priori* for countries with large populations where the potential for innovation, once users/consumers are identified as sources of innovation can easily be enhanced. In doing so, innovation is less driven by the continuous search for quality improvements, typical of the old mode of technological progress, identified with the high-income groups in society, but by broader user needs across society. These needs are also evident in the poorer, bottom, or base parts of society."

NOTES

1. Freeman, R. (1976). *The Overeducated American.* Academic Press.
2. Tinbergen (Jan. 1974). Substitution of Graduate by Other Labour. *Kyklos*, 27(2).
3. For more recent analyses see a.o. Sauer, P., N.D. Rao, S. Pachauri, March 30, 2015. *The Race Between Education and Technology Revisited: An Integrated Approach to Explaining Income Inequality.*

Sabu Thomas

I strongly believe that start-ups are the strongest engines for wealth creation, employment, and development. Start-ups in Kerala are about creating prosperity. Many enterprising people who dream of starting their own businesses lack the resources to do so. As a result, their ideas, talent, and capabilities remain untapped—and our state loses out on wealth creation, economic growth, and employment. I am glad that our FinanceMinister looked into this issue very skilfully and made the required budget allocations.

Coming to the domain of skilling, reskilling, and upskilling, I am of the opinion that this is extremely important for the state. Probably you all know that, for any nation, productive and formal employment depends on the availability of a skilled labour force through sustained investments in skill development and entrepreneurship. Skill development and employability are interrelated. Universities and schools should teach life skills, technical skills, and soft skills. We should also provide vocational education, training schemes, internships, and on-the-job training. Students have to be taught excellent skills during their studies through internships. I can tell you the story of a great polymer chemist and a good collaborator and friend of mine in Belgium, Prof. Gabriel Goeninckx. He is a great polymer chemist, at the same time he is a great plumber, a great painter, and a great mason too. Professor Groenickx told me that he has learned all these skills during his college and school days. China's skilled labour force helps in boosting its economy. China has made several industrial parks in the universities. Hundreds and thousands of Chinese students are being trained in

---

Sabu Thomas, Vice Chancellor, Mahatma Gandhi University, Kerala.
E-mail: sabuthomas@mgu.ac.in

the science park at the universities and industrial units. My good collaborator Professor Yang Weimin, is a well-known polymer engineer, he is a consultant to many polymer companies in China. He gets a lot of funding by consultancy for the university. As a result, the companies grow, and ultimately, universities, faculty members, and students are benefited.

Let me talk about the incentive system in the universities. In Chinese Universities, if you publish a paper in *Nature*, they get 20,000 US dollars. I think we should also give some sort of incentives to our faculty members. So, we have to make dramatic changes. I think universities have a very big role in transforming Kerala into a knowledge-based society. Universities should be the centres for the production of knowledge; they should be centres for disseminating knowledge to society. Universities have to build up excellent infrastructure. They should interact with industry and society. I think Dr. Isaac has succeeded in that; he gave a lot of funding to universities through KIIFB. All our academic programmes should have well-defined in-built internships, as in Drexel University in the US. We should teach the students extra skills; and inculcate the power of creativity, critical thinking, and innovation. If you look at the Global Innovation Index, we are much better. We are actually ranked 50 in the Global Innovation Index. We should teach our students to take risks, and encourage them to ask questions, experiment, observe, and network. We should teach the students how to manage and plan multifaceted projects. Universities should have incubation cells, and science parks as in China. If you look at the American Chemical Society (ACS) statistics, 80 per cent of the products that you see in the market are spin-off from the universities. I think we should transform universities into excellent places where knowledge is transformed into value-added products.

Finally, I think Kerala has never witnessed such a beautiful budget giving tremendous thrust to higher education. The Finance Minister tried his level best to strengthen our universities in a big way—by building massive infrastructure, and providing faculty and post-doc positions. If you look at the GER of Kerala, we are actually behind Tamil Nadu. The GER of Kerala is 37 per cent and that of Tamil Nadu is 49 per cent. I request Dr. Isaac that we should try to build a GER of 75 per cent for Kerala, how can we do that? We must really build up excellent schools, we do not need any newer universities, but under each university, we should have excellent schools, departments, and centres. Look at the student strength of our university campuses, it is less than 2000. If you look at leading universities in the world, the strength is 25,000, 50,000, 1,00,000... and so on. If you look at the University of Pennsylvania (UPENN) in the US, the strength is 80,000. So, we need to have excellent schools/departments/centres at the universities, we need to have excellent colleges, and we need to have state-of-the-art polytechnics and ITIs. We also need to have excellent nursing colleges, paramedical colleges and if you can do that, definitely our GER will go to 75 per cent. I am sure our higher education can do extremely well if you look at these points carefully. Thank you so much. It was a wonderful conference. And I am very happy to cooperate with Finance Minister and your team in all your endeavours.

Thank you, Dr. Isaac.

Judith Sutz

The budget document is an evidence-based policy proposal, oriented by a normative vision convergent with Sustainable Development Goals. One of the strengths of such a document, in my opinion, is that it is rooted in what Kerala has achieved so far, in its traditions: it is not one more of those wishful-thinking texts that pile goals without much contact with reality. Of course, another strength of the document is the clear identification of difficulties and constraints to go along the proposed road. This said, I would like to make five points.

1. As is rightly put in the document, universities need to be part of the effort of transforming Kerala into a knowledge society. Of course, quality is of paramount importance here. However, assuring quality is weakly related to international rankings. These rankings fulfil a very precise role: they are the commercial showcase of higher education systems that have evolved towards business services. Quality is not always measured by the number of publications in high-impact factor journals. There is an international effort going on to change the prevailing research evaluation system, DORA (Declaration on Research Assessment). In my opinion, such change is fundamental for what Kerala is aiming to achieve. International comparisons push researchers to work on problems that are of interest to international journals; this orients research agendas away from problems of local importance but with little visibility in the northern countries.

Judith Sutz, Professor, University of the Republic of Uruguay & Former President GLOBELICS. **E-mail:** jsutz@csic.edu.uy

The stress of achieving a number of papers leads also to addressing short-term, little risky problems, and even to pursuing inadequate conducts, like "salami papers". I would love to work with Kerala researchers to help build a new global academic reward system, convergent with open science, where no important problem is left aside and all research is carefully assessed in terms of quality.

2. The document puts the overcoming of the digital divide in a correct perspective, away from a sort of magical thinking by which digitalization by itself will solve all problems. Digitalization may bring more dignity to people if people already have it: housing, sanitation, good nutrition, health, and general education need to be there to allow digitalization to deploy all its potentialities. The recognition of social problems in Kerala, including inequality, and the impressive list of measures to address them pave the way to a digitalization process that adds to development instead of transforming it into a new sort of mirage.
3. To help the revamped knowledge system of Kerala address the whole gamut of problems that require new knowledge to be solved, some problems and demands need to be unearthed. This is so for various reasons, including that people may not know that knowledge can be of help for solving some problems, or that they do not know how to phrase a problem in knowledge terms. Unearthing knowledge demand beyond "strong knowledge actors" is not an easy task. But when knowledge demand is clearly stated, research, particularly local research, answers. A Uruguayan anecdote illustrates the point: a team of young researchers at the University of the Republic started developing a new clinical test for COVID-19, combining different pieces of evidence in an innovative manner. They did that for two reasons: rich countries would overbuy test kits; they also wanted to provide a cheaper solution that is available in the market. Their success was impressive. They provided a key piece in the strategy pursued by Uruguay in the first six months of the Pandemic. When *Nature*, in the issue of December 24, 2020, included Gonzalo Moratorio, the young scientific team leader, as one of the 10 scientific personalities of the year, the whole country was thrilled. This reaffirms the conviction that when demand is clearly stated, it may deliver innovative solutions. My group at the University Research Council has developed a methodology for unearthing knowledge demand related to social inclusion problems: we would love to put our modest advances at your service.

4. Innovation and development scholars have learned from India the concept of frugal innovation. This leads to paying attention to the heuristics followed to solve problems, to the need for creativity, to the acknowledgment that never ever there is a single solution to a problem, even if this is what we are told. The mantra of "do not reinvent the wheel; if someone has already solved a problem just buy the solution" etc., is misleading. Re-inventing by following different heuristics is simple good common sense. Developing frugal heuristics to problem-solving, that is, innovation, is something in which we can be of service to humankind. I am sure that Kerala could excel in that.
5. Governments have urgencies of all kinds; they need to show results in the short-term of politics. However, these urgencies need not take all their efforts. A small protected space, a sort of niche, where pursuing demand unearthing, where heterodox heuristics to solve problems are followed and tested, may always be allowed. Perhaps, among the wide array of Centres of Excellence that are envisaged, a Centre for Heterodoxy in Innovation (or something like that) may be included, centred around problems defined differently and solved differently. You have been so audacious in your document that a proposal like that can perfectly fit in.

Jayati Ghosh

It is always inspiring to be involved with the Government of Kerala and Dr. Thomas Isaac, in particular, because of that combination of vision, ambition, energy, and commitment. I hope Kerala continues to be an example for the world. In the spirit of your excellent Budget Speech, which has outlined so many different things that I think at some point, you mentioned this list is not exhaustive. One that I really want to emphasize is the translation services. You know this is something that has always amazed me that in India we do not do more. If you look in Europe, they have translation even for 3,00,000 people. They will have complete translations of everything.

There is so much scope for translation from Malayalam to English and from Malayalam to Hindi and back, which is very important for inclusion because it allows every citizen of Kerala and every resident to have access; It allows your migrants to have access to your work, it allows people outside Kerala to know of what is happening in Kerala. It allows people in Kerala access to all kinds of knowledge. It is very undeveloped and one of those things that happens only when you provide it because people do not know what they are missing otherwise. Once you generate it people realize what they are missing and that becomes a demand which is the answer and you get a market for it. But there is a real need to establish a translation mission that would translate everything, not just literature but scientific work, economic and political weekly. I mean, all kinds of things and work done in Malayalam to be made available to a wider audience. So, my first plea would be to put a translation. It is also very employment-generating, particularly for skilled labour.

Jayati Ghosh, Professor, Jawaharlal Nehru University, New Delhi.
E-mail: jayatijnu@gmail.com

My second point is about the recognition, dissemination and promotion of traditional knowledge. You already have a very excellent IPR policy, I think in 2008 you did that for traditional knowledge. But I do not think there has been enough follow-up in terms of actively looking for codifying writing up and disseminating the traditional knowledge. So, I would again put the emphasis on recognizing and disseminating traditional knowledge as a major area of activity. Related to that, in a way, agricultural extension has really lost out in India. There was some attempt to revive it in the late 2000s. But since then, whether it is agriculture or other primary activities, fisheries such attempts have been sadly missing. We do not have enough relevant research. Relevant for the problems that producers are facing today and relevant extension, especially when people have to face climate challenges, new pests, new kinds of things etc. you really need much more emphasis on knowledge pertaining to agriculture, fisheries, forests, and dissemination and extension services related to that.

Then there is Kerala's huge advantage in care services. You already have tremendous skill and experience in a whole range of services. I think you are ideally placed to develop new kinds of things in care; geriatric care, Alzheimer's, dementia, or palliative care. Kerala is now in a position to go beyond basic health care to new kinds of care. These are globally much more significant because of demographic change and greater incidence of various kinds of trauma and various kinds of disorders that need active intervention. Once again, I do not have to emphasize this is very employment-generating.

Finally, I just want to mention that you talked about how each of these things is going to be decentralized and the local governments will have an important role to play. I really think you should be looking not only at the mission mode that Mariana Mazucato has been talking about, but also at the doughnut approach that was popularized by Kate Raworth, which is being used today by the city of Amsterdam, Barcelona, and others. And that is looking at creating sustainable cities in which you can actually bring together various forces of knowledge to make sustainable cities that are also human creative cooperative democratic. I think there is a huge potential in Kerala because you are beginning on a much better place. You are beginning on a base in which you have a highly educated population, relatively speaking, not higher education, but in general, everyone is educated and you have a much greater civic awareness. So, the potential for doing that kind of doughnut economics is to create sustainable cities that are also fun to be with and good to live in.

Arun M. Kumar

It is no surprise that the recent budget by Dr. Isaac has placed the creation of a knowledge economy as its centrepiece. I am very glad to see a focus on higher education, that is foundational to a competitive knowledge economy. The proposed creation of a knowledge economy fund, ensuring ubiquitous access to the Internet and advancing the use of AI and the Internet of Things are all transformational initiatives that you have laid out. Many talks today reflected the fact that the quality of thinking and innovation in Kerala is already many steps ahead of other parts of the country and in fact many parts of the world. My remarks will highlight a few thoughts on Kerala's efforts to establish and successfully execute its ambition to be a knowledge economy.

First, I want to highlight the importance of and applaud the state's efforts to promote an ecosystem that fosters the digital industry. The ecosystem should help the state ride the wave of the fourth industrial revolution that is well upon us. The ubiquitous availability of connectivity is leading to the democratization of technology; Dr. Isaac asserted his commitment that there shall be no digital divide in Kerala. The state, with its high human development indicators, is uniquely poised to take advantage of the paradigm shift of the fourth industrial revolution.

The state is a pioneer in terms of creating a proactive policy environment, being the first in the country to formulate a policy for the development of technological start-ups and incubation centres. It is important to continue to evolve this enabling ecosystem.

Arun M. Kumar, Chairman and CEO, KPMG. **E-mail:** arunkumar1000@hotmail.com

Many successful Kerala entrepreneurs, who have made their mark globally, nationally, and regionally, can help lead this endeavour. Mention was made today of the important need for mentors. Successful entrepreneurs and experienced industry executives should be tapped in this regard, possibly with incentives for their participation.

My second point has to do with data. Along with ubiquitous connectivity, we are amid the Big Data revolution, the ability by which we can now process, collect, curate, and utilize what has been called a tsunami of data. To unleash the power that this presents, Kerala could consider embracing open data concepts which would allow citizens to review, compare, visualize, and analyse government data online and share their findings in real time. In my tenure in the US government, I saw how President Obama's policies for open data led to a host of new businesses that grew up to use such data.

Let me now come to the revamping of the skilling ecosystem to take advantage of the disruptions brought about by technology and by Big Data. Talent is becoming increasingly critical in proportion to capital as a factor of production, while robotics and AI are displacing human endeavour and repetitive work across sectors. Studies have predicted that up to 50 per cent of the current tasks and skills will be replaced by AI. In this regard, it is important to understand the near-term and long-term changes that are likely to happen and shape the skilling ecosystem accordingly.

A critical requirement today is to collapse the barriers between the specialized skilling institutions like the ITIs, and universities and industry. The legacy paradigm is that of training institutions that deliver programmes anticipating the needs of industry and then supplying graduates annually. But in this new era, skilling can no longer be episodic or modular and we must embrace a new paradigm of flexible, customized, and contextual lifelong learning. This means all the actors, skilling institutions, communities, and firms must work together as a coalition. And skilling delivery models can be asset-light, transmitting learning and skills even remotely, through media like the mobile phone.

The COVID-19 crisis has exposed two other disruptive trends that we need to be prepared for. Increasing talent and price arbitration arising from the ease with which skills and work can be delivered remotely to clients worldwide, and the rising popularity of what is called gig working—where services are increasingly being delivered to firms exogenously, and not by staff on the payroll. Kerala should tap into these opportunities and serve global clients working from Kerala, at a scale that surpasses what is already happening.

And last but not the least, leveraging the educated women population of Kerala. Kerala has a significant number of qualified women. Dr. Isaac mentioned the number of 5 million, who are not in formal jobs. In the wake of COVID-19, a number of remote execution jobs, from data analytics and predictive modelling, to design services for various industries that are suitable for women, are emerging. A focused attempt to make such opportunities available, along with a well-targeted upskilling initiative, can potentially double the formal working population of women in Kerala.

So, I will conclude with my belief that a new moment for Kerala is well within sight and the state can build on its favourable socio-economic base to transform itself into a knowledge economy based on soft skills, technology, and innovation—and commitment to inclusivity.

José E. Cassiolato

At least since the 1990s there has been a consensus that, with the development and diffusion of computer technology we are in the middle of an era where information and knowledge are the main tenets of a revolutionary period that affects all aspects of human life. In economic and social terms, we are witnessing a tendency towards the internalization of knowledge within the circuit of value.

The publication of the World Bank's 1998/1999 development report ("Knowledge for Development") opened the space for the definition and implementation of policies aimed at innovation and at the "knowledge economy or society". Based on the proposition that "knowledge, not capital, is the key to sustainable economic growth and improved human well-being" (World Bank, 1998), the report identifies the areas where "information problems are most acute" (*sic*), requiring government policies.

Following such proposals, in 2000, the European Union, under the Portuguese presidency, launched an ambitious project of economic and social transformation—the Lisbon Strategy, which aimed to transform, in ten years, Europe into a knowledge-based society. Founded on the Schumpeterian notion of systems of innovation and on the concept of a "learning economy", it aimed at a deep social and environmental renewal, better working and living conditions for the European population, higher levels of education and training, and a significant increase in investment and spending on Research and Development. Its ambitious goal: is to become *by 2010 the most competitive and dynamic*

José E. Cassiolato, Professor, Federal University of Brazil, RedeSist Coordinator & Former Secretary General, GLOBELICS. **E-mail:** cassio@ie.ufrj.br

knowledge-based economy in the world, capable of sustainable economic growth with more and better jobs and greater social cohesion.

To ensure the equilibrium between economic growth and ecological considerations, the Lisbon Strategy was completed with an environmental dimension. Thus, a new objective of sustainable development was introduced, based on the principle that every possible consequence is examined before a decision is taken. In this view, the focus is set on specific priority domains: climate change, viable ecological transport, health security and the reduction of polluted means *via* the responsible administration of natural resources.

The Lisbon Strategy set up important targets for 2010. For example, there was an objective of reaching 70 per cent of the general employment rate and another of every country reaching 3 per cent of GDP spending for R & D. These objectives were never achieved and on the contrary, all of these indicators went down. Social and environmental targets have also been missed.

In fact, social exclusion progressed, precarious work has spread like a plague throughout Europe, inequality augmented, and STI policies have not delivered positive results. In the environmental context, the Kyoto Protocol and its greenhouse gas emissions target are far from being implemented. Various forms of pollution have in fact been increasing in the last years.

Therefore, the happy enthusiasm of the beginning has progressively been replaced by the realization of the impossibility of meeting the proposed targets. There have several attempts to explain the failure of the strategy but perhaps the most and important direct reason was spelled out by Maria João Rodrigues, the Portuguese European member of parliament who was the main official behind the design of the strategy, during a Key Note Speech in the Globelics Conference in Athens in 2017. In a nutshell, she pointed out that although the strategy was designed within the Neo-Schumpeterian framework of Systems of Innovation, its implementation by the Brussels European Commission was made with Neo-liberal policy proposals. Much earlier, referring to the obvious failure of the strategy, Erik Reinert' at the first Globelics conference in Rio de Janeiro warned precisely that the use of the systemic notion of innovation European policy proposals that were rapidly spreading throughout the world were just "a new icing on an essentially neoliberal cake".

Since then, there have numerous attempts to devise strategies for the "knowledge economy throughout the developing world. Most of these attempts have failed, perhaps because they did not take into account the reasons for the intended results of the policies that have been unfulfilled.

The government's proposal of a programme for transforming Kerala into a knowledge economy is a welcome initiative but should reflect on these failed attempts and, certainly, on some successful experiences. Such reflection is even more important now-a-days as the world economy and politics have been so deeply shaken by a pandemic that nobody, after 18 months of its commencement, can predict its eventual end.

However, Kerala is in an excellent position to start such a venture. In the last 60 years, it has had extraordinary achievements in several areas that are necessary for today's world. It has impressive indicators in education and health—direct results of active state policies that are precisely the opposite of the neo-liberal prescriptions, excellent S&T infrastructure, and a production structure that even arguably modest proved its value during the difficult pandemic period.

The Kerala programme is anchored in three basic pillars—skills, infrastructure, and innovation systems—those that are precisely necessary. As a suggestion for reflection, I will comment on what is arguably a successful programme of a small country that was achieved under very difficult circumstances—economic, social, and geopolitical.

An editorial in *Nature*, Vol. 436, Issue 7049 (July 2005) stated: "Cuba has developed a considerable research capability—perhaps more so than any other developing country outside of Southeast Asia." Cuba has been especially successful in establishing a biotechnology industry that has effectively introduced drugs and vaccines of its own, along with a nascent pharmaceutical industry that has achieved considerable success in exports. Its agriculture and health sectors have been strong beneficiaries of the programme. As Nature observed: "It is worth asking how Cuba did it, and what lessons other countries might draw from it."

During the Globelics Conference in Havana in 2015, we learned a lot about the way Cuba set up such an initiative. In his speech to the conference Dr. Agustin Lage, its chief scientist, summarised the main reasons, precisely in the framework of the Knowledge Economy.

According to his assessment, the first is that the most important point of any strategy for a successful transition to a knowledge economy is that the workforce has progressively greater qualifications, motivation, and creativity and that society as a whole is capable of providing the underlying cultural and educational basis for this kind of labour. The knowledge economy, therefore, requires much more than the application of new knowledge and techniques in the high-tech sectors. More fundamentally, it also demands that knowledge, education, motivation, culture, and creativity penetrate all of productive society in a conscious and self-reinforcing way.

He also pointed out three traits that he considered to be essential to Cuba's success. The first one is that the entire process of the successful innovation system is integrated within research-production-marketing centres. The principal Cuban biotechnology centres were built as research-production-marketing centres where the complete cycle (encompassing research, the production process, domestic distribution, and international marketing) is housed in the same administrative unit. In this manner, the often-artificial barriers between scientific institutions and factory work have disappeared, resulting in a rich flow of information where commercial and production considerations are brought into the process.

The second is that export orientation coexists with domestic demand and distribution and international cooperation. Recognizing that in small countries' context, the domestic market is not large enough to cover the high fixed costs of R&D and quality control systems, export orientation would be an essential precondition of the programme viability. However, the internal market—and the role of the government's purchasing power is also essential not only to serve as a learning space but also in order to guarantee stability and visibility of future demand. Such obvious linkage between inward and outward orientation is even more important now-a-days given the uncertainty surrounding the world economy and the present, correct, perception of the relevance of "short circuits".

Finally, he mentioned the importance of treating, from the point of view of the government's budgets, the whole process, including particularly S&T, as an investment and not an expenditure.

His final remarks are worth mentioning: "The neoliberal ideologue is mistaken (intentionally or not) in assuming that market forces will promote economic productivity and that this will ultimately generate social development. It is out of solidarity, altruism, and a sense of justice that we invest in education, culture, and the development of our human capital. It would be naive on our part, however, to assume that this investment will spontaneously result in a fruitful interaction between S&T and the economy the and development of material production based on knowledge and high technology. The process is not spontaneous—it must be directed."

A year and a half after the start of the pandemic, it can be said that the world economy and society are faced with 3 scenarios. The first denies the seriousness of the pandemic and states that 'normality' will return soon, even though around 4 million people have died so far, some of them unnecessarily. The second recognises the seriousness of the pandemic by proposing adjustments in the public policies in place in Western countries (especially in health) but rules out structural changes. As the Prince of Falconeri stated in the book Il *Gatopardo* by Giuseppi Lampedusa: "Everything must change everything to stay as it is." The third, on the other hand, recognises the importance and urgency of the measures proposed by the second, but points out their limitations, emphasizing the need for structural changes and showing the unsustainability of the current modes of production, consumption, and life. The three scenarios—each of which offers a narrative of pandemic adjustment to be the only possible one—would represent the terms on which social and political conflicts will play out in the immediate future.

In the research that I, together with Prof. Helena Lastres, conducted with the country's most important research institution in the area of health (Oswaldo Cruz Foundation), we found that the acute crisis of the pandemic accelerated several processes, especially the use and potential of digital technologies (Industry 4.0). We observed a number of positive experiences that proved to be economically, socially, technologically, and politically viable in the context of the pandemic. More found at the territorial level, these most successful experiences in dealing with the crisis managed to escape the false health-economy dichotomy and aimed to endogenize the productive and innovative capacities of different strategic activities, allowing a rapid industrial reconversion and the establishment of the so-called "short-circuits" where activities essential to life in the territories themselves are offered and consumed.

These experiences are in line with the third scenario mentioned above, highlighting the urgent need to put the State and its policies back at the centre of the necessary transformation processes. From this perspective, the well-being of the populations inhabiting the different territories of the planet is placed at the centre of any development project, of structural change and, therefore, of the new policies, especially those aimed at the knowledge economy, such as that of Kerala. Some countries are already moving towards putting well-being and health at the centre of their strategies. Not surprisingly, those that have been most successful in meeting the challenges of the pandemic are those that were already moving in this direction, or those that quickly discovered the importance of doing so. Perhaps the most emblematic example is New Zealand, whose government, as early as late 2019, had sent to Parliament a government budget proposal focused entirely on the well-being of its people (The Well-Being Budget). Kerala's proposal regarding the Knowledge Economy is an excellent opportunity to achieve a reality that points to the future of human survival.

Gabriela Dutrénit

I would like to focus on one specific aspect that I consider important to ensure success in the dynamics of this transformation: the evolution of different sub-systems of society that influence the decisions and actions that are taken. As the Minister described, this process presents the arenas of economy, technology, and innovation. But our countries are complex and are at the stage of development where the problem of social inclusion is a key issue in any strategy, as was mentioned by many colleagues before. Hence, other sub-systems of society may be included in consideration.

I would like to go back to Chris Freeman, who in 1995 told us that a set of sub-systems of society are important in the process of change, namely science, technology, economy, politics, and general culture. Freeman provided a different lens on how to analyse the development process and which components should be included in a strategy. Some sub-systems like science (which includes ideas, individuals, and institutions) could be more important than knowledge of engineering and math as Patrick Heller said. Technology includes artifacts and techniques, but also the activities of the individual, groups, and institutions involved in the design, development, improvement, and diffusion. The economic sub-system includes institutions concerned with the production, distribution, and consumption of goods and services, and those individuals and institutions concerned with the organization of these activities. But the other two sub-systems mentioned by Freeman include politics and the general culture. Politics include ideas, non-values of individuals and institutions concerned with

Gabriela Dutrénit, Coordinator, Management and Innovation Policies, Metropolitan University, Mexico City, Mexico. **E-mail:** gabrieladutrenit@gmail.com

the government and the governance, and the legal and political regulation by the central, local, and international authorities of society, including military affairs. And also, Freeman mentioned the general culture. I mean ideas, values, artistic creations, traditions, and knowledge that were mentioned before. This includes education, which is an important aspiration of Kerala. Coming from developing countries, but also from what we are leaving today in the world, we have to add two other sub-systems. One is the social aspect that is much a problem of the developing countries concerning income distribution, inclusion, and the generation of social welfare, but we also have to add the environment, which Freeman did not include at that time in 1995 but for us now is a must.

Each of these sub-systems of society has some independent performance, but they interact and influence the process of economic growth. Hence, it can either emerge from a lack of synchronicity or harmony between the sub-systems when you are analysing a process of change, or in contrast, they can converge and generate a virtuous cycle effect on economic growth and development. Hence, what is key with the sub-systems of society is not only that they evolve, but also that they interact and co-evolve. However, the success of a process of economic growth and development is associated with the extent to which the changes in these different autonomous sub-systems of society are congruent instead of counteracting each other.

What we have seen in our countries is the lack of congruence between the political institutions that come from the past and the advances in the economy related to the Internet of Things or manufacturing 4.0, or the contradictions between the high rate of growth and the persistence of high level of exclusions, hence the distribution of benefits of the economic growth is unequal. And now during COVID-19, we have seen in several countries, an interesting response from the business sector, particularly the small and medium enterprises and even the informal sectors, with the emergence of new practices, services, and products, which denote greater entrepreneurship and innovation than before. In most of the countries, this behaviour has overcome the government measures and incentives showing a different evolution of the sub-systems.

So as a final reflection, I would like to say that the transition of Kerala to a knowledge economy might require elaborating strategies that consider the different sub-systems of society. It is needed to better define which are the relevant sub-systems in the case of Kerala, and analyse how the policy can contribute to the evolution of these autonomous sub-systems. It is important to identify clearly which institutions are relevant, how institutions favour positive bi-directional links, and where to make an investment to strengthen these links between different sub-systems. It is relevant to reflect on how to analyse the relationship between sub-systems and also to identify the existence of thresholds in any of these sub-systems that affect the evolution of the country as a whole. Hence, we need to design policies that include instruments to promote a synchronous and harmonious development of all the sub-systems.

We are excited to know and follow up on these interesting processes that happen in Kerala and can be an example for many other developing countries. Thanks for the opportunity to give an opinion about what is going on in Kerala.

Patrick Heller

I have been learning from Kerala and, in particular, learning from Professor and now Minister, Thomas Isaac, for almost three decades. So, it is an absolute honour and privilege to be here. I will take the opportunity to comment on the budget and maybe locate it in a larger context.

So, let me begin with a brief comment about the literature on accelerated economic transformation. That literature focused on the developmental state. But today we are talking about a very different kind of a developmental state, that is, the 21st-century developmental state which is geared not so much to promoting industry, but rather services and a knowledge economy. In thinking about the 21st-century developmental state, I think there are four features of success that we have to underscore, all of which are present in the Minister's budget speech.

The first is having and articulating a specific vision and associated projects grounded in local history and politics. The budget does just that by specifically framing the idea of developing a knowledge economy as an extension of Kerala's overarching democratic project. Second, is having the actual state capacity to get the job done. By state capacity I do not just mean the conventional focus on bureaucratic and technical capacity, but also the ability to coordinate across governmental agencies and in particular coordinate across levels of government, especially local governments. Third is a focus on expanding human capabilities -both for their intrinsic value of sustaining human freedom and their instrumental value for supporting development. Fourthly, we need states that are

Patrick Heller, Brown University, Director, Development Research Programme at the Watson Institute of International Studies and Public Affairs.

E-mail: patrick_heller@brown.edu

not just democratic, but that are deeply embedded in civil society. And by civil society, I do not just mean movements and associations, but also autonomous institutions of knowledge production, most importantly universities. So, let me just make three substantive points along these lines, and then finish with a comment about universities in particular.

In many respects, Kerala is the prototype of the 21st-century developmental state. It is building on its extraordinary achievements in welfare and capability enhancement, but also in deepening governance specifically by deepening democracy and empowering local governments. There is now an abundance of comparative and historical evidence to suggest that the key to promoting more inclusive forms of economic dynamism is local government.

The second point, again, building on the successes of Kerala's long-term investment in welfare and capability enhancement is precisely finding new ways to leverage those investments. The two fastest-growing sectors in the world are education and health. They are labour intensive, especially as the nature of care itself intensifies and education specializes. There are extraordinary opportunities here to build on those welfare state investments. But I think the key here—given the tendencies towards precarity and fragmentation of the labour force and the growth of the gig economy—is ensuring that there is security for workers in these new highly flexible work arrangements.

Let me then quickly turn to higher education, which is of course the new thrust of the Minister's budget speech, and here I just want to make two points. First, the budget speech, of course, is about broad-based commitments. Next comes the actual detailed programmes and the devil is always in the details. I think one of the details that really needs to be thought through carefully is the question of the autonomy of institutions of higher education and there is reference to this in the budget speech. But, for those of us who have experienced working in universities in the United States and Europe, we all know that one of our institutional advantages is the extraordinary autonomy that we have as faculty and as researchers. And I think that is not always been the case in India. Preserving autonomy from market forces, but also from the state itself is essential to attracting the best and creating environments of innovation.

And then let me make my final point that goes to the information economy, but also the particular role that higher education will play in supporting that economy. In an environment of scarce resources, there is a tendency in the debate on the new economy to emphasize technology and innovation and in doing so to prioritize STEM (science, technology, engineering, and mathematics) disciplines at the expense of other disciplines. But the knowledge economy is not just about technology and innovation. It is also about creativity and in particular understanding how the digital interfaces with the social. Creativity today is rooted—more than ever—in culture. And I think it is absolutely essential to invest in cultural capital, to invest in pedagogical models that are inter-disciplinary and that ground hard knowledge or technical knowledge in the social and cultural fields.

Let me finish by observing that given Kerala's long-standing history and success as a people-centric model of development, it is uniquely positioned to build a knowledge economy, but not just any knowledge economy, but rather a knowledge economy that would be more cosmopolitan, more pluralistic, more inclusive, and more deeply rooted in a very creative culture. Thank you. And again, it is a true honour and privilege to be part of this conversation.

Susan E. Cozzens

The Budget for Kerala for 2021-22 is a bold document, laying out a distinctive pathway towards shared prosperity in a changing global economy. Kerala has long been a model for human-centred development; this document continues that commitment. The foundation of Kerala's social cohesion has been its investment in the health and education of its people. This new stage of development is possible because of that investment.

Nonetheless, key questions remain, as raised in other contributions to this volume. Kerala for what? Kerala for whom? Whose knowledge will count? Can Kerala continue to sustain "proactive equality" and build a knowledge economy?

Inequality in High-Technology Economies

These questions are critical because of what we know about the dynamics of inequality in high-technology development. High-technology development produces high-skill, high-wage jobs; this is inherent in its design. Typically, the number of such jobs is small in relation to overall employment. In countries with low general levels of education, most people do not have access to those jobs because they are not prepared for them. Fortunately, that would not be the case in Kerala. The people who hold high-wage jobs are able to support the service economy around them—laundry, retail, food, transportation services etc. These are typically low-wage jobs. Thus, the high-technology economy adds fewer jobs towards the top of the income scale and more at the bottom; this increases inequality.

Susan E. Cozzens, Professor Emerita, Georgia Institute of Technology, Atlanta, GA, USA, Vice President, GLOBELICS. **E-mail:** scozzens@gatech.edu

Inequality is already rising very fast in Kerala. While its human-centric commitments give it among the lowest levels of poverty among Indian states, it has the highest level of inequality. Inequality increased by ten Gini points over the period 1994 to 2005, quite a remarkable increase seldom seen in the world statistics. These Gini numbers are consumption-based; increases in income and wealth inequality are probably even more dramatic.

Strategies for Spreading the Benefits

There are some key elements in the Knowledge Economy strategy for Kerala that will help to protect social cohesion in the face of these income and wealth dynamics. The commitment to preventing a Digital Divide is one. Additionally, and perhaps surprisingly, the expectation that Knowledge Economy work will often be done from home is another, in ways that might not be immediately apparent. When people can do their high-wage jobs on a distributed basis, they will also support local businesses with their spending. Neighbourhoods can maintain a mixed-income, mixed-use character. Mixed-income neighbourhoods make it easier to maintain high-quality public schools for everyone; high-income families are less likely to flee to private schools and low-income families have access to the education that underpins social mobility. Children from different kinds of households go to school together, know each other, and are more likely to participate as equals in "the democratic project of Kerala". Kerala surely does not want to bifurcate.

In building a distinctively Keralan knowledge economy, some other lessons from the state's history are important to keep in mind. Local, craft knowledge has long been a font of innovation in Kerala, like the knowledge of farming and fishing. This will not only be important in bottom-up innovation in the informal economy of the state, but also needs to be combined with more formal knowledge. Innovation that is suited to a broad range of economic circumstances is generated best when people solve problems using expert and local knowledge together. Kerala's egalitarian social environment should be rich soil for this type of growth.

The massive investment in infrastructure that appears in the budget can also be the site of distinctive innovations. For example, Kerala's water supply is under stress, in ways that other regions are also experiencing. Inventing and implementing ways to address such challenges could be marketed elsewhere by Kerala-based enterprises. Likewise with innovations in energy, health, and transportation that are suited to Kerala's conditions. These can result in products that can be exported to markets that European and American firms do not understand, along with the approach of adapting them locally through local knowledge and experience.

Keeping the Wealthy in

Through all these steps forward in shared innovation and shared prosperity, wealth will accumulate. It is essential to "the democratic project" of Kerala to keep the wealthy in. On the one hand, Kerala's leaders should keep a close watch on tax structures, to make sure that the new wealth that accumulates is shared back into investments in people, the kinds that have made Kerala fertile ground for a Knowledge Society. On the other hand, leaders need to exhibit the attitudes and mutual respect that will hold the community together.

With its strong, community-oriented leadership, Kerala will surely be able to forge this unique way forward.

A.V. Jose

To me, sitting right through the webinar, was an immensely rewarding exercise. It was the kind of an immersion course in a whirlpool of ideas, floated by people from far corners of the world, all directed towards making Kerala a knowledge economy, not just for its inhabitants, I believe for the whole of India. The knowledge setup that develops in Kerala ought to be meant for the rest of India. I am confident that we have the visionaries prepared to underwrite the cost of embarking on such a venture. We have the skilled craftsmen or the knowledgeable persons who can make it happen, chart out every step involved in turning an idea into a product, and reach it to the market. It is a very ambitious venture that has been planned in the context of Kerala. I do believe Kerala is ideally suited for that because it is just a continuation of the transformation process, we have had in the past involving the democratization of the public space in the education and health spheres.

What happens next is the sequential stage of generating a knowledge economy, where knowledge is made accessible to people at the lower end of the income distribution. It is a natural consequence of our past development and I am happy to note that the state has embarked on that in full force. The budget document is a clear indication that the state and its political leadership are prepared to go to any length to realize that vision. The fact that the Finance Minister said in the morning session: "forget about the cost or the mobilizing resources, I am going to make it happen, I am going to ensure that the resources are there" is a profoundly significant statement and indeed one of the most rewarding experiences while listening to the whole discourse here.

A.V. Jose, Former Director, GIFT. **E-mail:** avjose11@gmail.com

What I wish to say is that in Kerala, the focus is now shifting to the service economy. The service economy, by the way, is significantly different from the one we have envisaged as centred around manufacturing activities. We might have a difference of opinion about the relative importance of different industrial divisions. Maybe 10 years down the road, we will still be focusing on manufacturing, but the shift is entirely towards the services sector based on the use of skilled labour. This is the culmination of a new industrial transformation where work is moving to where the people are, unlike in the previous industrial revolutions where people always moved to where the work was located. Therefore, making the instruments of skill acquisition accessible to people at the lower end of income distribution is extremely important. That is being pursued in Kerala.

More importantly, they are trying to make it possible for women workers to come into the labour force, which Professor Sushil Khanna made a reference to earlier. What needs to be done is to make sure that the reserve prices of women in skilled labour households are met through what the state has to offer, which means it has to create an ambiance to make work far more attractive. This means that more than raising wages, which is part of an all-India process, we should focus on establishing appropriate institutions for social security. This is not just for the distribution of the state's largesse but for the creation of annuity-based contributory pension funds, which is what has been emphasized in the budget document. As the Finance Minister mentioned earlier in the day that he is going to meet the cost of social security payments for all the new jobs being created outside the public sector, it is indeed one of the most commendable initiatives.

Another point that Professor Khanna raised again in this session is about raising the quality of higher education. This has got to be done with the involvement of the existing crew of teachers and professors. I have heard the point often raised by very responsible people, familiar with the higher education setup, that nothing is possible with the existing crew. No, that is not the case. The point is that they have to be empowered to enhance their skill sets and move up the ladder by making it possible to interact with the best and the brightest in the academic community in the rest of the world. This again is eminently doable. We are moving into the service economy and there is an abundance of opportunities awaiting us on account of the income effect generated through the factor price equalization theorem becoming fully operational. And that is something that Kerala can certainly look forward to. All those people passionately involved in planning for the future and charting every step in the transformation, I wish them the very best and look forward to working with all of you.

Thank you very much.

Alexandre Oliveira Vera-Cruz

I am grateful for the opportunity to learn from the experience of Kerala and be able to express some words related to this strategy of development based on knowledge. I would like to make a point only on the topic of public policy, specifically on public participation in this process, and the public policy challenge of transforming Kerala into a knowledge economy.

The decision regarding the design of STI policy in our countries has dominated a top-down approach, an approach to government policy as opposed to public policy. Therefore, there have been difficulties in recognizing the voices of stakeholders. Government policy faces the challenge of becoming public policy and for these, the participation of interested parties is required. The public nature of the policy refers to increasing stakeholders' participation in the policy formulation process. Public participation is a political principle or practice. It can be recognized as a human right, the human right to public participation. It can be seen as a form of empowerment of citizens and there is part of the democratic governance. In order to design a public policy, it is required to think in participation, negotiation, and consensus generation of proposals of the different actors of the STI sector. To deepen public participation requires fostering the dialogue between officials and stakeholders for the decision-making process.

Public participation in STI opens space for a dialogue between STI communities (stakeholders) and the officials. Each community intervenes with different intensity in each stage of the policy cycle. The evidence at the

Alexandre Oliveira Vera-Cruz, Professor, Metropolitan Autonomous University, Mexico.
E-mail: averacruz@laneta.apc.org

international level shows more intense participation in the stage of definition of the agenda and design, which is the stage in which Kerala is.

Today, the generation and management of the dialogue is part of the governance capability of the national innovation system. I believe that public participation is very important for this strategy of development based on knowledge with the vision of transforming Kerala into a knowledge economy. We are very interested in this process that you are starting now and I am confident that it will be an example for many developing countries.

Thank you very much.

Jeffrey Orozco

Okay, first a thank you for the invitation. It is an honour for me, and for Globelics to be part of this activity. I think it is very important for you and also for us in Globelics to stress the relevance of our global network. It gives some feedback on these development challenges. There are also many lessons from Costa Rica, but I do not have the time now to say something, especially from our agricultural sector, on how to manage their R&D sector, their diffusion of knowledge, and also, the attraction of investment. Since you are about to be at your midnight in India, I am not inclined to elaborate on any of these aspects. But I am sure later on, we will have a number of opportunities for more intense, elaborate, and relaxed discussion.

For now, just to think about this activity and to remember that we are having a Globelics Conference this year in Costa Rica. We have already sent the call for papers. We hope to have a hybrid conference with some people here in Costa Rica and others online. It will still be difficult to predict how the situation with COVID-19 will be by the end of the year (November). But I think this activity is a good example that we can share and the technologies help us to share in different ways. I thank everybody, we had a lot of feedback from experts from everywhere. It is really an honour for Globelics to be part of this and I hope that this dialogue will continue. I look forward to welcoming all of you in person in Costa Rica for the conference, if not, at least online.

Thank you.

Jeffrey Orozco, National University of Costa Rica & Secretary General, GLOBELICS.
E-mail: jeffrey.orozco@gmail.com

Index